Self-Help Sucks

The Anti-Self-Help Guide to
Inner Peace and Contentment

Tony A. Blankenship

For Alicia and all the mentors, spiritual and otherwise, I have had in my life.

Contents

Author's Note

Are you tired of reading fluffy self-help books that do not really deliver any lasting change in your life? Have you tried, time and time again, to change your behavior through your own willpower only to find the harmful habit intact?

I had the experience of committing to a twelve-step program and it changed my life. So complete was the change that I began picking up so-called self-help books when I came face-to-face with the inability to change other behaviors in my life. While the writing was fantastic and the marketing was exceptional, the books' advice failed to enact any real change, even though I really gave it my best effort.

After hitting a wall and becoming so miserable that I slid into depression, I decided to apply those same twelve-step principles to my other problems. This time, the results were amazing! Not only did I stop doing the thing I did not want to do, but I also caught glimpses of a type of contentment that I had never experienced.

This book is about that experience. It's a simple six-part program built on those steps, borrowing from their principles and my personal experience. What follows is a guide to daily living that has and does work for me . . . and I believe it will work for you too.

This book is for you if you have tried other self-help methods and found them lacking and full of fluff. This book is for you if you have a behavior in your life that stubbornly persists, no matter how hard you try to leave it behind. And some of what you experience within these practices may surprise you. This discovery has led me to a relationship with God, something I never thought could be possible. In many ways, this is a guide to contentment and purpose, which works if you put in the effort. .

Something told me to write this book, though I do not know what it is. I refuse to give it a name, but I believe it will help you as it has helped me.

After sending off my first attempt at writing a book to a highly respected publishing house, I woke up with this overpowering thought. I couldn't shake it, and nothing else could get into my mind. I could not get it to go away.

I sat and did my daily meditation, trying my best to stay spiritual, for God's sake. But I kept hearing this voice. "Tony, write this book," it said. "Here is the title. Start today. Don't wait—write this book."

Being who I am as a person and all, I asked, "What about the other book I just wrote that needs all this work; doesn't that story need to get told too?"

No answer.

Two minutes later, the voice repeated, "Write this book … Start today."

OK, Universe, I will do it.

"It better be good," I thought.

I invoked "the Muse" as I do every time now when I write, and I started typing.

Author Stephen Pressfield wrote a book about resistance and how to break through called *The War of Art*. (Please read it. The book was so helpful, and his realistic point of view is encouraging.) In it, Pressfield notes that a "professional," and that starts with a frame of mind, simply does the work that needs to be done. After reading that, I sat down and did what needed to be done. The rest is up to the Universe, the gods, and those who might use this book to help themselves and ultimately help someone else. That service is the purpose of this book.

I pray it provides for my family and me, but no matter what, I knew I had to write it, regardless of where it leads or who it touches.

Thank you in advance for reading it. I love you.

– Tony

Introduction
Self-Help Sucks!

Do you have something that you can't stop doing in your life? Gambling? Online shopping? Screen addiction? Are you a control freak? Are you addicted to emotionally unavailable people? Have you tried self-help methods to stop doing these things and failed? Are you tired of reading fluffy, empty, and wordy books that offer no real change? Me too.

I tried every self-help approach out there. I spent thousands of dollars and countless hours creating vision boards, repeating affirmations, and just trying to exert plain old willpower. Every time, I'd find myself in the same hole, one more time—and that's when I realized self-help sucks! It's BS! It doesn't work. It never did, and it never will.

We all want to go out and exert our power of

will and get stuff done. Make things happen. Change ourselves, our habits, and our behaviors. What I am telling you is that *self*-help sucks. I mean that on our own power, without the help of a Higher Power and the support of others, we will not be able to change ourselves.

If you are a person who wants to change something in your life or are in a twelve-step program and wants to deepen your program, this book is for you. Filled with exercises and meditation and prayer, it lays out a foundation for daily living that is beneficial for everyone.

In this no-nonsense twelve-step-based guide, I have laid out a path based on my own experience. I offer the same practices that helped (and continue to help) me achieve a sense of inner peace and contentment and freedom from these habits and behaviors.

After several years in a twelve-step program, I came face-to-face with my inability to change what I was doing. I was making myself miserable and hurting people in my life and knew I needed to find a solution. I picked up several self-help books and, even though the writing was excellent, none of them provided the change I so surely wanted in my life. Having worked the twelve steps in the program I was in, I decided to apply those steps around the behavior I was struggling to change. What happened was amazing! It not only freed me from this destructive behavior, but it also provided me with a sense of contentment and inner peace I had yet to achieve, even after twenty-two years in a twelve-step program. I continue to apply this process to the things that pop up in my life. It has never failed for me, and that's why I feel called to share it.

There are upwards of forty twelve-step fellowships globally that have helped millions of people overcome their addictions and destructive behaviors. The steps work. Period. It is by no means an easy system, and most people must get beat up badly to fully submit themselves to it, but I have personally never seen anyone who is being honest and has done everything it asks them to do ever not get better.

In the chapters to come, I'll share my experience with the process of the twelve steps in the original six-step format that was followed at the beginning of its history. Included are a few other people's experiences doing the same thing. All of us have one thing in common: we came face-to-face with behaviors that we could not stop doing on our own. We all worked the steps, and came out on the other side free from the behavior and with inner peace and contentment. It is by no means meant to be a replacement for a twelve-step program or your spiritual practice. It is only my experience with what I did.

Before we begin, there are a few things I'd like you to know:

When you start to do this work, begin each day with a prayer (or your own version of a prayer), asking the power to set or lay aside all that you think you know.

Start with five minutes of meditation every morning! Later in the book, I will cover an approach to meditation, but for now, imagine a beam of light in the middle of your forehead and put your focus there. Thoughts come and go, and that is a natural thing, so do not worry yourself about it. The important thing is that you carve out the time to do this first thing in the morning. Do the same thing consistently, every day, no matter what.

Get a notebook that is only for this work. Keep everything together in an organized space. There will be exercises and meditations that will require you to write down your experiences as you go along.

Finally, I will talk a lot about God in this book. It is not meant to convey any specific religion or viewpoint—the truth is I consider myself a spiritual agnostic. What I mean by that is I have no idea what God is. I just know that it works. Use whatever is the most accessible to you and what makes sense in your heart. Words are wholly inadequate and cannot convey what that Power really is, so do not worry about semantics. Give it a chance and do everything suggested here, and you cannot fail to get results.

Dear Divine Spirit, (use whatever description you like)*, please set aside everything I think I know about myself, about my story, about my* *problem* (insert problem: money, sex, etc.)*, and especially about you, Spirit* (use whatever you like)*, so that I may have an open mind and a new experience with myself, with my story, with* (my problem) *and with you, Spirit. Please help me to see the truth. Amen.*

Say this prayer every day when you get up in the morning. After which, move into five minutes of meditation or quiet time. Use the method of picturing a beam of light in the middle of your forehead. Thoughts will come and go. Let them. When you begin to get distracted by a particular idea or story, focus back on the light. You can also focus on the diaphragmatic breath in the same way you focus on the beam of light. If you already have a meditation practice, add the prayer above to begin or to finish your time, whichever feels right.

Chapter One
Powerless: "The Evil I Do Not Want to Do"

"I do not understand what I do. For what I want to do I do not do, but what I hate I do.
Romans 7:15

We all have something in our life that torments us. Even Paul the Apostle struggled. As he wrote about it in the Bible, "For I have the desire to do what is good, but I cannot carry it out." I'll bet that, at some point in your life, you have tried on your own to change that destructive behavior without help. So have I. And I'll bet you have failed repeatedly. I've done that too. This chapter is all about what happens next, and we'll begin with a question that may make you feel uncomfortable.

What is it in your life that you have no power over? What is that behavior you have repeatedly tried (and repeatedly failed) to change? Look, I get it. No one wants to admit they are powerless. No one wants to think that their willpower is weak and they can do nothing to change the circumstances of their lives. It is a hard truth to admit or even consider.

It could be a career you are stuck in, shopping, relationships, sex, the internet, or repeatedly doing something you do not want to, no matter how hard you try to not do it. Apostle Paul called his problem "the evil I do not want to do," and I think that is a helpful way of describing it. Better yet, let's put it into a question: What is it in your life that you keep doing, no matter how hard you try to stop?

In this chapter, we look at three elements of powerlessness:

1. Once I start, I cannot stop.
2. I make up my mind not to do it and do it anyway.
3. My life, especially around this problem, is unmanageable.

There are two things I want to make clear before we go any further: If you are grappling with behavior in your life that obliterates you, something that eats you up and spits you out—whether it is drug or alcohol addiction, relationship addiction, porn, sex, gambling, food—if you are struggling with something that's destroying your relationships, family, career, home, health, or self-worth, go join a twelve-step program. Work through their steps, do everything they say. You will come out on the other side not only victorious over that thing but with a whole new set of ideas and a way of life that is very fulfilling.

The other thing is that if you do not really want to stop doing what you are doing, or you just kind of want to stop, this is not for you. You must want it bad enough that you are willing to be challenged in a way that you may not have been challenged before. You will have to look at things that will make you uncomfortable and tell someone else about them as well as go out and make amends for the harm you have caused in your life, especially around this behavior or problem that you have named, and declare that you are ready to try something totally opposite of what you think might work. Whatever that thing is, make sure you really do not want to do it anymore. With the help of whatever Power you identify with as a Higher Power, make the commitment to do whatever it takes to go down any road this work leads you down.

Once I start, I cannot stop.

I have ulcerative colitis. It is an autoimmune disease in the large intestines and the bowels that causes inflammation in your digestive tract. That inflammation causes "flares" that put your waste system into overdrive. You can get uncontrollable diarrhea striped with blood and mucus, lose your appetite, and become anemic from blood loss. When you are in a flare, you always must know where the nearest bathroom is and stay close to it. Because you know there's no stopping *it* once it starts. Because if you are not in the bathroom when it comes, you will either go in your pants or find a nearby bush. No matter what your intentions or how hard you try, you still shit your pants. That's true powerlessness, and addictive behavior works about the same way.

The concept of "once I start, I cannot stop" was first introduced to me as step one in the twelve-step work that I did. There is almost an allergic reaction. Here's an example of what I mean. Let's say you are walking in an alley and you see that someone has thrown away a half-eaten chocolate cake. You tell yourself, for some reason, that you would like to have a taste of this chocolate cake. You tell yourself you are only going to have a couple of bites. You pick up the cake and eat your two bites, then put the cake back on the ground where you found it and walk back out to the street. However, you suddenly feel a compulsion to go back to the alley and eat some more cake. You make your way back to the alley and polish off the whole thing, making yourself sick in the process from eating not only a whole cake but eating a cake that was left out in an alley.

One of these things for me was continuing to chase and get in relationships with emotionally unavailable women. I would see a woman across the room or in a crowded space, gravitate towards her, and ask her out to coffee or something. We would go out on a date, and very quickly, I would know in my heart that this person was not going to be able to show up for me. The writing would be all over our interactions, and I would make up my mind that I would not continue pursuing her and would instead wait for the Universe to bring me who was supposed to be in my life. Yet, a couple of days later, I'd be calling her to ask her out again. In a very short time, I'd somehow manage to take another emotional hostage and end up with yet another failed relationship I knew would not work from the beginning. I could see it; I would watch myself do it, and I'd watch myself try to stop. I gave myself speeches in the mirror. I read self-help books. And even though I knew something was wrong with me, and despite all my effort, I could not change—no matter how much I wanted to or needed to. I just kept engaging in the same behavior over and over, feeling guilty and remorseful every time I did it. I was powerless, but I was not willing to admit it until it almost ruined my life. This leads to the next aspect that we look for in being powerless, which is the most insidious part of the problem.

I make up my mind not to do it and do it anyway.

Now let's say you disgusted yourself with your inability to stop eating the cake once you started eating. You have cleaned yourself up and made a very sound and meaningful decision to not eat chocolate cake ever again. You never want to find yourself in that situation again. It makes sense. You are a bright, willful person who has willpower in most other areas of your life. You do not overspend or gamble, and most of the time, you show excellent judgment in your life. There is really no evidence or reason why you should not be able to fulfill your decision.

Hours lead to days, and days lead to weeks, which lead to months. You haven't thought of the chocolate cake at all. If you have thought of it, it repels your senses so much you have almost vomited thinking about yourself hunched over the cake in the alley. One day you walk by a bakery, and right there in the window is a freshly decorated chocolate cake. It has chocolate sprinkles and chocolate truffles on it with chocolate ganache and chocolate buttercream frosting. You find yourself standing at the window staring at the chocolate cake. It's like your feet are glued to the cement; you cannot move. Suddenly you find yourself at the register paying for the chocolate cake. You walk outside and sit down on a bus bench right in front of the bakery. The cake just starts going in your mouth. There is no thought, there is no memory of the alley or your decision; there is only the chocolate cake in front of you being shoved into your mouth. That is what it's like to have a mental obsession. No matter how hard you try to remember how bad you felt, or maybe you had a great day and decided to celebrate your success, you find yourself breaking your word and wolfing down cake repeatedly, no matter how hard you try not to.

In the twelve-step program that I worked to change my life the first time to overcome addiction so powerful and destructive it rendered all the fat off of my body and burned every relationship down to the ground, I grappled with this type of mental obsession. And it reared up again in my relationship choices when I would pick out the most unavailable (at least to me) woman in the room.

Who was incompatible with me? I'd make a beeline for her, start flirting with her, give her unmitigated attention, flattery, and even gifts if that is what it took. I would pursue these women, get into a relationship with them, and convince myself that I was in love with them. (And maybe I was more in love with the idea of them or in love with being in love.) We would go along and more than likely move in together and even get engaged. I have done this more than once—and one of those women was a lesbian and knew she was a lesbian; she told me so. I still pursued a relationship.

Each of these relationships would follow the same doomed path: soon after we moved in together or got engaged, everything would start to deteriorate. The long bridge of differences would stretch wider and wider, like the Grand Canyon, until eventually we could hardly see each other from the other side. Both of us knew we weren't going to make the journey to reconnect across such a vast divide, and the end rarely came as a surprise.

The thing is, I knew it would happen that way. I knew if I went across that room and talked to *that* girl, we would follow the inevitable pattern. I also knew I would end up with a broken heart and a broken will, full of guilt and remorse. In the end, I'd be all alone with the wreckage of my soul's sickness scattered around me in ruins just as a tornado leaves a trailer park after it touches down on its path.

My life is unmanageable, especially around this behavior.

What does it mean that my life is unmanageable, and why is it significant to the condition of being powerless? I tried on my own to overcome this condition with self-help books, mindset exercises, therapy, and just straight old willpower, only to find myself stuck in my mind. Everything I felt was "wrong" with this world and its inhabitants grew larger and larger. I had a good-paying job, a girlfriend, a car, a place to live, clothes on my back, and all of my needs met, yet I continued to stay unhappy. I finally admitted to myself that the wrong thing was inside of me, and on my own, I could do nothing about it. Nothing changed. I needed help that was beyond me.

For me, it was a never-ending cycle I was doomed to repeat—making myself sick and trying as hard as I could to stop doing it. Every time I was single, I would become so negative and unhappy that I'd jump back into a relationship with someone incompatible with me, despite my commitments to myself to stay away from women for a while.

Below, I go into some of the conditions that I looked at within myself that make up an unmanageable life. All of these are internal conditions that have nothing to do with the outside world. These things would get so intolerable, so untenable, that the only solution for me was to go back to the behavior that gave me relief from the things I was feeling on the inside.

RELATIONSHIPS

Think about all the relationships in your life. How are you getting along with everyone in and around your circle? How are you getting along with the people in your job, in your house, and in your community? My experience was that everyone in my life seemed to be doing something wrong;

they were never doing enough (or they were doing too much). The people at my job were either incompetent or know-it-alls. My intimate relationships were a mess, or I could not commit to a healthy and loving one. If everyone in your life is doing it wrong, they may not be the problem. All of these relationships had one common factor, and that was me. I was the common denominator. What was wrong was inside of me. Because the truth is, even when they started doing things the way I wanted them to, I still wasn't happy.

EMOTIONS

Are you having trouble controlling your emotions? Can you regulate your reactions to people, situations, and inevitable life changes? Are your feelings dictating your actions and reactions? Can you predict how you will feel, or is it more like a yo-yo that bounces you around, up and down, back and forth, day in and day out? My experience is that when my life is in an unmanageable state, I cannot regulate my emotions, nor can I predict how I am going to feel. What is even more unmanageable is that I will then make decisions based on how I feel at any given moment. If I feel sad, I make a decision based on that. If I feel abandoned, I make a decision based on that and so on. As time goes on, this becomes worse and worse, and my feelings and emotional state bounce all over the place. Given enough time, it can start to look a lot like a mental health issue to an outsider.

BOREDOM

You are the victim of boredom, depression, and misery, even if it looks like everything is fine. You get up, brush your teeth, grab a bite to eat, and then you're out the door to go to work. You have no problems, except your boss is a jerk. Suddenly out of nowhere, for no reason, you feel sad, distraught, upset. I would walk around with an active bitch face, despite the fact that nothing discernible happened to make me feel this way. I just couldn't control it. I found this would happen more frequently the longer I went without the behavior I was trying to avoid, the thing I used as a Band-Aid to give me temporary relief.

FEAR

You are afraid. Afraid of what people think, fearful of what they are not thinking. Afraid of not getting what you want. Fearful of getting what you want. Afraid they will not be enough. Afraid of success. Afraid of failure. Afraid to start. Afraid to finish. Almost every single piece of your life is touched by fear in some way or another. The more it gets fed, the bigger it gets, and trying to just not be afraid on your own only makes for more fear. Bigger and bigger.

DISSATISFACTION

You are never satisfied with what you get. No matter what comes your way—a raise, a new car, a motorcycle, a mistress, a new job working for your dream company—nothing is ever good enough. Ever.

NEGATIVITY

More and more, negativity becomes the prevailing feeling in your life. I do not want to be like this. I want to be cheerful and happy. I want to be a positive, uncritical person to the people in my life and at work. Except I am a drag. I cannot see the good things in life, no matter what they are. The glass is always half empty; there are perpetual storm clouds on the horizon, and no amount of willpower or effort will make this go away.

This thing inside is like a spring with a crank arm that goes to the soul. If left untreated, it will get wrapped tighter and tighter. The inside of me is so sensitive, so reactionary, and so unhappy. It is constantly scanning the world, looking for that thing that has always given it relief, before blowing it all up. And then doing it again, *and again*, over and over, until I get so sick of myself that I can't even look in the mirror. When this happens, I am utterly powerless to do this on my own.

All of these things combined add up to me being powerless. Do any of them sound familiar to you? Take a look at all of these components in your life surrounding your behavior or the habit plaguing you, and look at your experience. Do not look at how you want things to be. Do not look at how things used to be in the past or how you hope one day they will be. Look at your experience now, today, when you do these exercises. In the twelve steps, the principle of the first step is honesty. It does not mean that all of a sudden, you are going to go out and live an honest life. Not yet. It means you will have to take a clear-eyed look at yourself and your current experience and ask yourself some uncomfortable questions. In this step, the questions to answer continually are: Can you stop doing this on your own? Can you make up your mind to quit and do it? All the time, not just for a minute. Can you manage your life on your own? On your own self-help program? That is the honesty principle at work. In the beginning, I asked you to start praying as I did. It is so crucial in this process. I cannot change these things on my own, nor can I really see these things on my own without the aid of a Higher Power. That is what will work for you too, but only if you do it.

Self-help sucks, but self-honesty is essential.

Get out a notebook, a scratch pad, or even just a sheet of paper. Grab a pen too. Write down any behavior that you struggle to stop doing on your own. Once you have your list, go through each one and answer the following question:

Is it just a bad habit that you can quit? Or is it something that is stronger than you, and no matter how hard you try, once you start doing it, you cannot stop? Place a mark next to any habit you cannot stop once you start.

Finally, look over your marked habits and answer this question:

Which is the hardest one to digest? Which makes you feel the most uncomfortable? Circle it.

Now, answer honestly: Once you start doing this thing, whatever it is, can you stop once you start?

Let's keep going. Can you think of three times that you decided not to do this behavior and really meant it? Have you ever promised someone else that you'd no longer do this behavior and really meant it? Write those instances down and be specific and detailed—and make sure you stick to the facts.

You see, your ego will fight this exercise

tooth and nail. It will trick you into believing that you do this habit because you decide to. Your ego will tell you that, no, you didn't really mean it when you decided you want to stop–or that you changed your mind. Or that it wasn't your fault, that it was understandable, that it wasn't a big deal. Your ego will spin stories to keep itself fed, which is why you need to stick to the facts as you make your list.

Here's another important question for you: Did you *really mean it* when you decided to stop? If you're like me, your answer may not be a simple "no" or "yes"; it'll look more like "no, no, no, no, yes, no, yes, yes." In my case, I prayed about it, talked about it, and went to therapy about it. I knew that it was killing me. I knew it was hurting the women I cared about, and that I was doing damage. I'd decide I was done with pursuing unavailable women, and I'd really mean it and would live accordingly . . . for a while.

After the wreckage from the "tornado" was cleared and the grass had started growing back and the homes were rebuilt, I would once again find myself in a room, a coffee shop, a meeting, church, or just hiking on a trail in the beautiful mountains of Santa Fe, New Mexico. I would spot her in the distance and completely forget my decision, forget the work I had done in therapy, forget that I really meant what I said.

It would be like watching myself in a movie from above, looking down on myself as I walked over to her the same way I did all the other times before. I would ask myself from up above, *What the fuck are you doing, Tony? You know how this is going to end. Did you forget how this ended last time?* I'd watch as the people who love me tried to call me back. *Not again, Tony. What are you doing?* It didn't matter. I would watch my body move as though pulled by the world's strongest magnet. I could not stop myself no matter how much I tried. I knew I was powerless.

Does this story resonate with you? Answer the following questions truthfully: When you decide to stop doing your habit, using all the willpower and mental muscle you have, do you still break your word and go back to it repeatedly? Do you think you can keep away from it? Or is your willpower broken in this area?

Now let's pull back a bit to acknowledge who else is impacted by your behavior. It's time to examine how your habit bleeds into your relationships, including the one you have with yourself.

Write down your current experience with the relationships in your life. How are you getting along with everyone? Is everything harmonious, even in your own head? Or are there problems popping up, first here and there, which lead to more and more issues in your relationships? Do I think I can change these areas with my own help and willpower? Here are a couple of stories from others about their experience with powerlessness.

Letting go of control Dev's story

What does it take to want to change? My story goes like this. I have a long history of wanting to have control over everything and everyone around me. My clothes are sorted by color in my closet. I make my bed every morning—even when I'm sick and going to get back into it. I really believe that if other people just do what I think is best for them, their lives would be great. I make lists of everything I need to do each day. I take these lists and break them into smaller tasks. Then I make lists for bigger projects. Then I sort these lists into separate lists by category. I want to make sure everything is organized so I can control every aspect of my life. These are outward representations of my inner thoughts and mad desire to control the physical world, relationships, emotions, etc.

Things out of my control happen . . . some people don't like me; my marriage falls apart, and I get a divorce; I don't get the job I want or think I deserve; my daughter has low blood sugar, has a meltdown, including screaming and throwing things and refuses to eat; my entire house floods; my back goes out, and I can't exercise (which helps me sleep and stay calm and positive), and I can't keep my house clean; someone I love dies. I've had all of these experiences and more! Like the crooner Frank Sinatra sang, "That's life."

My first reaction to life is to refuse to accept it as it is at this moment. So I get angry. I have temper tantrums like my daughter when she hasn't eaten for six hours. I throw things, yell at people, stomp around the house slamming *doors, scream at the top of my lungs in the car, push away friends, punch my steering wheel, act like an asshole towards the general public. I become depressed to the point of wanting to die.*

Okay, that's crazy behavior, so now what happens? First, I need to become aware that I'm thinking and acting like an insane cartoon character. Sometimes a friend points out my recklessness by asking what's going on with me or flat-out saying that I seem pretty pissed off. Other times I become aware when I break something I like, notice the looks I get from others when I say something nasty, or realize I'm yelling, in my mind, at someone who isn't there. I'm fully aware that something needs to change when I honestly say to myself, "I can't live like this anymore. I am in too much pain to go on like this." When I am stuck in this painful anger, whether it be for a night or a year, I need a solution—and usually pretty fast!

T's Story

I was a longtime member of a twelve-step program (twenty-six years). I had worked the steps many times on life in general and on individual issues specifically. Still, at twenty-six years into the program, I found myself addicted to casino gambling.

It had started as an occasional diversion that I would indulge in now and then, but it became over time a full-time obsession, to the point that I had to go to the casino every day. I would not tell my wife where I had been (a lie by omission). I would not answer my cell phone while at the casino because I was ashamed to have people know that I was at the casino in the middle of the day. This dishonesty bothered me a lot, but the guilt over lying could not overcome the obsession to go each day. I talked honestly to my sponsor about it and told him that I was afraid that this behavior could lead to drinking. He agreed with me that this was very dangerous and asked if I had prayed to have it removed (which I had every day) and then suggested various means to overcome the obsession, including going to Gamblers Anonymous, which I balked at doing because my pride kept me from wanting to be a newcomer in yet another twelve-step program.

I would talk to the people I helped in the

twelve-step program about "rigorous honesty" and share at meetings about honesty and feel like a hypocrite (because I was one).

I prayed daily to have the obsession removed, and it seemed the more I fought against it, the worse it got. I thought I had gone insane, and on one level, I had!

One of my mentors once told me that he had taken the numbers off the steps. I didn't understand that at the time, but that's what happened to me.

It was obvious that I was powerless over gambling, and my life was extremely unmanageable.

As you can see, your habit impacts, and even harms, more people than just you. And if it's harming them and it's hurting you and you still can't stop—well, you are powerless over this thing. And it's important to say so. On the same paper you've been using for this exercise, write: *I admit I am powerless over ____, and my life is unmanageable.*

Here is this thing in your life that has brought you to this place, and you're fed up with it. It has consumed you and eaten your lunch, so to speak. You know that if you start, you cannot stop, but find yourself repeatedly starting the behavior against your will. Once you start it, you cannot stop it, no matter how many books you read or seminars you attend. You cannot control it. You're plagued by an internal condition tied to this behavior—negativity, depression, fear, anger—especially when you are not engaging in it.

I admit I am powerless over ____, and my life is unmanageable.

I could not break my pattern until I was willing to try something beyond my own power of reasoning and self-propulsion. My will was broken. Nothing I had tried worked to stop me from doing this. Given enough time, my unmanageability drove me back to the behavior, making it more palatable until I did it again and repeated the cycle.

Here's the thing: we are not powerless over everything. I love ice cream. I love it in summer as well as in the winter. I love it, homemade and store-bought. I could eat ice cream every day, but I don't. In fact, I only eat a few bites several times a year because ice cream gives me terrible gas and keeps me up at night with an uncomfortable belly. I don't like being up at night as a windbag, which means I only eat it once in a while when I'm out of town staying in a hotel room by myself. That way my wife doesn't have to suffer through the night with me. I am not powerless over ice cream. But I was powerless over continuing to chase after unavailable women.

That habit chewed me up and spat me out. It took me out for dinner and threw up all over the house every time I did it, and I could not stop no matter how hard I tried. No book, no workshop, no seminar could get me to change. Had I not done the work in this book, I would probably still be doing it. This book will challenge you. You will have to work. But if you're ready—if you *really* mean it—the practices in these pages can and will absolutely change your life. But I've got news for you: we cannot produce the change needed to overcome it ourselves. And that's what we'll be discussing next.

Dear Divine Spirit (use whatever description you like)*, please set aside everything I think I* *know, about myself, about my story, about my problem* (insert problem: money, sex, etc.), *and especially about you, Spirit* (use whatever you like), *so that I may have an open mind and a new experience with myself, with my story, with* (my problem), *and with you, Spirit. Please help me to see the truth. Please show me the truth about my powerlessness. Amen.*

Continue to practice your quiet time in the morning, now increasing the time to seven minutes.

Chapter Two
Surrender: Change Your Heart, Change Your Situation

"There exists a mystic power that can transform your life so thoroughly, so radically, so completely, that when the process is completed, your own friends would hardly recognize you. And, in fact, you would scarcely recognize yourself. It can lift you out of bed and free you to go out into the world to shape your life as you will. It can throw open the prison door and liberate the captive. This Power can do for you probably the most important thing of all in your present stage: it can find your true place in life and put you into it. This Power is really no less than the primal Power of Being, and to discover that Power is the divine birthright of all men." – Emmet Fox

I would like to tell you a story about surrender. I cooked for a living for thirty years. I have worked as a chef in one form or another since 2004, when I graduated from culinary school. When my daughter Hazel was born in 2016, I was an executive chef at a well-known local restaurant in Santa Fe. I was at work all the time, sometimes working twelve to fourteen hours a day and always working all the family-centered holidays such as Mother's Day, Easter, Christmas Eve, and Thanksgiving. My family would be at home celebrating together, and I would be at work at the restaurant helping all the customers celebrating with their families.

I am not really sentimental about holidays and honestly have some trouble with the history of them. It triggers my trauma. But I value quality time with my family, and I missed it because I was working this job. I was becoming unhappier and unhappier. I would get home and complain to my wife constantly and was grumpy on the days I could finally be home with them. My wife lovingly suggested that I find something else to do for a living, to which I replied, "Where am I going to make the kind of money that I make now?" followed up by "I can't just let this go." I was so unsatisfied with my work, but the days wore on, and I just kept holding on.

One January morning, I finished riding my bike on the trainer, and something came over me. I had spent my entire training session obsessed with my job. It was horrible. I got off the bike and said this prayer: "God, please change my heart or change my situation. I can't do this anymore." Two days later, I got fired and it was the best thing that has ever happened to me. That moment of surrender led me to this book, to you, and to hopefully helping you to make your own decision and find your own version of the Power that has changed me so much. I know it can change you too.

If we cannot change something within ourselves, it must come from somewhere else. Once I realized and accepted my dilemma, my powerlessness, I had this sinking feeling in my chest. It was as though I was standing out in the middle of a lake with no life jacket or help anywhere near me—and

I'm not a strong swimmer. I came face-to-face with the truth: I needed something else besides me to change me. I had to have some help, and it needed to be something far more powerful than me. *Self*-help sucks because it's not enough. It wasn't for me, and it probably isn't for you—and that means we have to talk about God, the Power.

Here was my problem. I didn't want to bring God into it. I had all sorts of old ideas that I had heard from other people, movies, church, books—or just made up in my own head—that prevented me from connecting to the idea of a Higher Power. No way was I going to turn my life over to someone else's God. I adopted these ideas from other people, from Sunday school, from movies, including one particular film about the rapture that I saw as a preteen that really messed me up. Most of these ideas were usually that I was not good enough for G-d. I would either go to some burning, fiery place or never get any help when I really needed it.

I had to find something that made sense to me and me alone. So I took out my notebook and described all the qualities I needed in this

Power. Each person can do this for themselves. It may seem blasphemous, but I can assure you it is not. What do you need for it to work for you? In your notebook, write down every quality that you desire in a Power greater in yourself. Some of the things that resonated with me were: *creation, universal power, best friend, all-powerful creative force, an accessible divine force, can change me.* These qualities are not defining God; they are simply laying a framework to give me something that makes sense to me. You get the opportunity to do this for yourself.

There are so many ways for each of us to approach this step. For example, it was important to me to use my own words and terminology to convey what I wanted. Some people may want to go to a church, go into a room, sit at an altar, or just be in their house at their kitchen table. Go where it feels right for you, where you feel the most connected.

You can also go outside for a walk in nature. Go to the woods, the river, the lake, mountains, parks, grassy fields, or even just around your neighborhood. Just go. Turn off your phone, turn off your music, and start to walk at a gentle pace. This is not meant as exercise; it's a pleasant stroll. As you begin your walk, say a prayer or, if you wish, an earnest request to open your heart and your mind and lay aside everything you think so you can have a new experience. Walk for thirty minutes. At the end of thirty minutes, stop, sit down, take a breath, take another breath. Look around you.

What do you see? What do you hear? How do you feel? Close your eyes, keep breathing. Are the birds singing? Are the leaves rustling in the breeze? What else is happening? Take five minutes to sit there on a rock, a tree, or a bench and breathe. Keep your eyes closed. Listen. What is in your heart? When you are finished, go back to your car or your house or where you started and write down on a piece of paper what qualities you need God to have to make sense to you—just you, no one else. Write them down. They can be things like creation, infinite love, energy, forgiveness, or inner peace.

Once you've compiled your list of qualities, ask yourself, *Can I turn my problem over to this Power?* (Or, if you're like me, *Can I turn my whole life over to this Power?*) Am I willing to give up my old life for a new one, knowing that I cannot create a new life on my own? If the answer is no, okay. Keep doing what you are doing and living the way you are living. If your experience is like mine, you may end up here again, and you can try again if you are willing. I made countless resolutions and had innumerable discussions, even with God, but I never truly decided. Once I truly faced the experience of being powerless to change, even though I desperately wanted to, I knew it had to come from something bigger than myself. I had to let go of my old ideas about this Power and come up with something that worked for me. The difference came once I identified God as having the qualities I needed from a Power greater than me.

All those other times, I wanted God to be a fairy godmother and come in with a magic wand and wave it over my head and magically change me without any effort on my part. I wanted to just ask and be changed. But I did not do any meaningful work once I made my resolution. How about you? Are you looking for a Power that can help you or a fairy godmother?

I looked at those qualities I had written down and asked myself again, based on my experience, did I think that I could change the way I behaved on my own? Could I just try harder? Could I, again, decide to change and do it? Was it ice cream, or was it something more powerful than me that I needed help with? The answer for me was that I needed help.

So, I decided that God, my Higher Power, would direct my life from here on out, that my Higher Power could use me in any way it wanted for whatever it wanted. I asked the Power to come into my heart and remove the obstacles in my way so I could do the work that needed to be done for it to change me. Because I knew I could not do it myself. You are welcome to use those exact words, or use your own, so long as you voice it without holding back and mean it as much as you can. God, the one with all the qualities you need it to be, will answer.

I had an experience when my daughter was born that I will share here. Your experience with God will be unique to you, but maybe my story will resonate with you and encourage you to look for yourself and find what works for you.

Shortly after my daughter Hazel was born, I pondered the Universe and such things as how long it would be before she pooped again or threw up on me. Out of "nowhere," I had this sudden realization: I could not make this being. I could not combine my wife's egg and my sperm, put it in a controlled environment (a uterus), and feed it in an underwater world through a tube that goes to its belly. I could not make it grow and develop and come out into this world an amazingly beautiful, screaming, pooping, gurgling mess. In fact, no human has ever been able to do that, and they have been trying for a very long time.

I realized, maybe for the first time, that something much bigger and more powerful than me made this beautiful creation, and the same thing could be said of really almost anything in this world. There is a Power, an energy that makes up all things, that connects us, even the tiniest things in this world. I had an inkling of it before, but never at this level. To this day, when I sit with that Power every morning and pray, it is that Power I am praying to. I trust that if it can make something so magnificent as Hazel, then it can indeed have enough Power to change me.

I do not think it matters what you call this Power. There are so many names for the Unnamable, for this Power, that have been used for longer than I have been on this planet. Use your religion if that makes sense to you, use nature, the Universe, the Power of the Universes—use whatever makes sense to you in your heart of hearts. Do not worry. The Power I talk to and sit with every day is always available, all the time, no matter what. If it is available to me, it is available to you.

This decision will not do much if you do not follow it up with constructive and meaningful action. So, having made the decision and genuinely committed to it, you must be willing to take a hard look at yourself and your stories and be ready to talk about it with someone.

Dear Divine Spirit (use whatever description you like), *please set aside everything I think I know about myself, about my story, about my problem* (insert problem: money, sex, etc.), *and especially about you, Spirit* (use whatever you like), *so that I may have an open mind and a new experience with myself, with my story, with* (my problem) *and with you, Spirit. Please help me to see the truth. Please show me the truth about my powerlessness. Amen.*

A prayer of surrender:

Dear Divine Spirit, I offer my life to you to do with as you see fit. Take away my selfishness, take away my unmanageability, so that freedom from them will show others that I will help your power, your love, and a way of life. May I do your will in everything that I do. Amen.

Continue your morning quiet time, increasing it to ten minutes, incorporating either this surrender prayer or your own prayer daily.

Chapter Three
Inventory: Examining Your Life

"For the unexamined life is not worth living." – Plato

"You can never truly understand or really help others, even in your own family, unless you first look thoroughly into your own life and deal with your own sins without compromise, excuses, or evasion." – John C. Broger

Any business with a rotating inventory of goods must keep track of them in some way, or the business will lose money and invariably fail. They must know what they have in stock to order more goods, and they must know what they have sold to have any accuracy in calculating profits. It is the same principle that propels the motivation to take an inventory of ourselves. Without being willing to look at the things in ourselves that have kept driving these destructive behaviors and habits, you will be doomed to repeat them. They will continue to manifest in your life. I believe that I was spiritually sick. I needed to get well spiritually, and taking an inventory of myself was the path toward getting there.

Why would I want to write down on paper all these seemingly private things that I really do not want to look at or talk about to anyone else? The truth is, for me, it was not enough to want to change, nor was it enough to try on my own power using self-help methods to produce the change that I wanted in my life. I had to look at the patterns and things in myself that had been getting in my way. The only way I have been successful at this was by writing an inventory. This principle aligns with the twelve-step program, and it has worked for millions of people to overcome so many things. If it works for them and can work for me, it can work for you. We are not trying to recreate the wheel or come up with a unique and separate method.

In the inventory process, we will look at our

resentments, our fears, and our relationships—which, admittedly, are all the areas in my life that seem to cause all my "problems." When I previously thought about the people I was angry at, I viewed myself as a victim and could only think about what they had done to me and dwell on my hurts. Taking inventory challenges that position. We are asked to brush aside or forget everything we think someone else has done and review our own behavior solely.

In the past, when I tried to do this, my inventory mainly consisted of what I thought these people had done to me or, more accurately, the story of what I thought they had done to me. I was never willing to look at my side of things. I only wanted to stay a victim, and a victim cannot get well. I am not saying I was never victimized. I was, and it had a massive impact on me and how I operated in the world. I am talking about making everything in my life someone else's fault or using what they did or what I thought they did as an excuse for my own actions. It is not them; it never was.

I cannot stay a victim and get well. If I remain a victim and my behavior continues to be their fault, I can never get well. I can never escape the cycle of my powerlessness. My decision was a significant part of my life. Still, if I did not follow it up immediately with a constructive, honest look at my life and behavior, it would have had no lasting effect. I had to look at myself.

We need to examine three areas of life, to get them down on paper and take a constructive look: resentments, fears, and relationships. If, for example, your powerlessness is over shopping online, the resentment might be at yourself for doing this repeatedly. Anger came first for me—anger at the people in my life or my grievances. I held resentment for my parents, bosses, coworkers, exes, and the people I owed money to (which is pretty funny, come to think of it). I had anger about God, other people's beliefs, and especially about myself.

I made a list of all the people I was angry at and why I was angry. I kept it simple and straightforward without getting drawn into the story in question or why I thought they did what they did. Then I looked at my beliefs about myself for each of these people and saw, really, that these stories and ideas I had were running my life. I was always thinking of myself and what they did wrong or what I believed they did wrong, and I was really getting sick of myself. Then I looked at what I did to them and realized that I could not overcome my anger on my own, that even looking at how I had treated people was not enough for me to get over it. I believed, and still believe, that to harbor anger at someone is a soul sickness that will always eat us alive. I needed a new plan.

Based on my experience, I know I cannot escape from this anger and resentment on my own. While writing these things down is helpful and useful and helps me to see my responsibility, by itself, it will not create the freedom that we so surely desire. I had to have help beyond myself. So I went to this newfound conception of my Higher Power and began to pray for the people I was angry with in earnest. What happened was amazing. I began to be free of my anger. I stopped playing the victim and started to take responsibility for myself. It is the path toward inner peace and contentment. I asked God to show me that the people who supposedly harmed me were, in fact, sick, just like me. To show me how to have forgiveness for them as I would want forgiveness for myself and to be free of my anger and how to love them and all people. I said this prayer every day I was writing. Without me trying to or setting my mind to a new mindset, my heart softened toward these people. I began to see that in their own way, they were doing the best they could at that moment with the tools they had been given in their life, just like me. That we were all the same. We lied, we cheated, we hurt people, we were selfish, and at the same time, we were loving, kind, and compassionate. We all, as human beings, had the same qualities and were showing up with the same stuff.

My ego always wants me to be better or worse than people. It still wants me to be the best motherfucker in the room or the worst piece of crap there is. It can never just let me be human; that is like death to my ego for some reason. But I believe that I cannot harbor anger in my life. I cannot get better spiritually if I am walking around with anger in my heart. It is also impossible for me to get rid of this anger on my own or by using self-help. I needed something bigger than myself to help me.

I said this prayer for the most prominent resentments I had as I looked specifically at what my actions were toward them. Where had I been selfish? Where had I lied (even to myself) about what happened, the role I played, and my responsibility in the situation? Which faults were mine? What harm did I cause? I asked this for every person on my list. What became clear to me, especially in these relationships I kept getting into, was that I knew these women were wrong for me the moment I saw them. I would have a gut feeling that they were the wrong person with the wrong kind of values for me. Yet, I would pursue them relentlessly to get my fix even after—or maybe *especially after* is more accurate—they would tell me that they were the wrong person for me.

The next thing I looked at was my fears. Every piece of my existence is connected to fear in some way or another. It impacts almost every area. Like the anger, I could not simply just try harder to make my fear go away. In fact, the harder I attempted to not be afraid, the more scared I was. It is the essence of a self-fulfilling prophecy. The more I focused on not being afraid, the more terrified I became. I am not talking about a fear of spiders. If the fear of spiders keeps me from leaving the house to go buy food to feed myself and my family, then I should probably go get some therapy for it.

What I decided to do was to look at my core fears—my deepest, most secret fears that kept me up at night and touched almost everything in my life, including my reactions and my interactions with people. Going back to my continued powerlessness with picking the same women repeatedly, what were my fears behind that? Some examples for me were:

Fear of vulnerability,

Fear of being seen,

Fear of being myself,

Fear of really showing up,

Fear of really having to love, and the list can go on.

When I boiled a lot of them down, the biggest, most destructive, corrosive fear was my fear of not being good enough. It shaped my reactions, placed me in positions to make decisions that I did not want to make, and drove me to take jobs I knew I did not want. The response to this fear has also torn apart relationships, forced me to move, quit jobs, and pick women who are utterly wrong for me. The worst thing I have ever done due to this fear is gone against my inner voice when it speaks to me.

How do you, as the reader, find out what your core fears are? Start by making a list of fears that come to you on the next clean sheet of paper in your notebook. Once you have those fears written down, do a boil-down exercise. For instance, in my case, I was afraid I would always continue being attracted to women who were unavailable to me. To boil down fear, you ask yourself progressively what is behind each fear. My fear was that I would never find a person just for me who I was compatible with. Keep going until you can't break it down any further. I was afraid of never finding someone, of being alone forever, afraid there was something wrong with me and that's why I would never meet someone, afraid God wouldn't help me, afraid I was not good enough.

There is a voice that is inside of me that tells me things. I have heard this voice my whole life. It might say something like, "Don't buy that from that sales guy. He's ripping you off." Or it might tell me to keep my distance from someone or let me know that they are lying to me. It had also told me it was okay to trust someone or to take a chance and take a risk I would have never taken before, or that I was supposed to help someone when I did not want to. Do you have something like that inside of you? I would guess yes; I think we all have it. It may be blocked off by all kinds of distractions and doubts, but I believe it is there for all of us. Do you know when the voice is speaking to you? Can you hear it when it whispers? When it whispers or even when it yells at you, can you listen to it? Can you follow your heart where it leads you? Or will your fears keep you from listening, and you'll go where you have always gone, down the well-worn path with the stones smoothed out, and the movie still ends up the same. Repeatedly, I have gone against myself and what I knew inside to be the thing I am supposed to do. But this fear of not being good enough overpowered me. It steered me toward the same empty places, empty beds, pointless jobs, and reacting to life because I was afraid I was not good enough for something better. I also knew in my heart that everyone else knew I was not good enough too. Why would my dream woman be attracted to me? Why would my dream company offer me the job I have always wanted? Why would the Power that I call God care for me and protect me, let alone love me, if I wasn't good enough? And on and on and on.

Let's walk through the fear exercise and what to write down, using my example of the fear of not being good enough. I use this for every one of my fears. What am I afraid of? Why am I afraid? What selfish behavior am I using because of this fear, and how am I not trusting my Higher Power when I have this fear?

I am afraid I am not good enough. I am so scared I will never be good enough and must settle for whatever I can get. I am selfishly taking whatever I can get because I am not trusting and relying on my Higher Power to bring me what is truly in store for me.

In my case, I look at the sexual and intimate

relationships in my life. This can be difficult, especially for those who, like me, use sex as a validation tool or take emotional hostages by using sex selfishly and dishonestly. These are your morals and values you are looking at, no one else's.

If you are not engaging in that type of behavior, ask your present conception of the Power to show you who in your life needs to be on this inventory. Write the names down. I have done this many times and had as few as three names on there. I usually include God on the list since it is the relationship I would like to cultivate the most and the one about which I have the oldest and unhealty beliefs. Once I get it all written down, I look at my selfishness, dishonesty, inconsiderateness, jealousy, or bitterness. How should I have treated them? Be hard on yourself. Dig deep—this is a chance to see how you are behaving in your life relationships.

Finally, I looked at these relationships and prayed about how I would like to behave in the future. What principles would I want my relationships based on? Which would I like my sexual relationships based on? As I asked how

I should have treated people, it laid the foundation for a framework I can use every time I interact with people. In my case, I wanted honesty, vulnerability, integrity, and a spiritual base to all my relationships, sexual or not.

One of the other things that came up for me is that, though I am married, I really like women and the attention of women. I like flirting with the girl at the counter at the deli. I like it when she smiles at me, and I like the brief fantasy I have when she gives me a particular type of smile. I mean, I really like it. However, it is not honest. It is inconsiderate to my wife, and if she were doing that with an attractive guy at the counter at some deli, I would feel jealous and angry. So, one thing on my list is that I do not flirt with other people. I do not operate in a way that would cause my wife harm, make her jealous, or give someone else the attention that should be going to her. I asked the Universe to shape my ideas and help me to live up to them in the way I wanted to live up to them. To help me treat each person in this world the way I wanted to be treated. To remove my fears so I could see that the people I thought had wronged me were perhaps just sick like me, and to save me from my anger and show me how to help them in some meaningful way.

Remember, through all of this, keep praying. Keep meditating. Ask for help from the Universe, Allah, Buddha, Mother, Jesus, Jeshua, Jehovah, the Ancestor, Love, Christ, or whatever makes sense to you. Ask it every day. Because *self*-help sucks.

Here is what to do. Write down your resentments and old ideas about yourself, such as "I will never be good enough" or "unlovable."

The notebook is open, and the left-hand side of the paper is my belief system: When I was angry at my wife for not giving me what I wanted, it affected

My belief about who I am: I am the greatest husband.

What I want: I want her to always tell me I am the best and give me what I want.

What I need: I need to get what I want.

My friends and family: Should always give me what I want.

Sexual relations: Women always give men what they want, and men always get what they want.

Money: If I have enough money, I will be happy and satisfied.

On the right side of the paper:

Selfish: I selfishly always want to get my way and for my wife to give me my way.

Dishonest: I am dishonestly expecting her to always give me what I want. I think getting what I want will satisfy me or make me happy.

Afraid: I will not get what I want, and somehow my wife not giving me what I want means that I am not good enough.

What is my responsibility? Always insisting that I get my way.

Faults: Selfishness and demanding.

On the next piece of paper, I write my fears and use the example from earlier: What am I afraid of? Why am I afraid? What selfish behavior am I using because of this fear, and how am I not trusting my Higher Power when I give in to this fear? What would my Higher Power have me be? After getting all of this down, I ask my Higher Power to remove my fears and show me what he would have me be.

Next, I look at the sexual and vital relationships in my life. I usually include myself and God on this list. For each person, I ask myself: *Where was I selfish, dishonest, inconsiderate, or caused jealousy or bitterness? How should I have treated them?*

When I get all those questions answered, I look at them and prayerfully come up with a set of principles that I want all of my relationships to be based on. Some examples of that could be honesty, faithfulness, spirituality, stability, and respect. Write those down for yourself. From here on out, and with the help of the Power you are praying to, live by those principles to attract the same qualities in the people in your life.

The last thing I consider is if there is anything else I need to look at. Are there any secrets I'm keeping or any behavior that I know I should not be engaged in? If the answer is yes, I write these things down and am ready to find someone out there to hear all the stuff I have written down.

If you have been thorough in this step, you have written down some hard things about yourself, and you have looked at your anger, fears, and most intimate relationships. If you are like me, you may have asked yourself what all this has to do with becoming free of a desired behavior or habit. You may be thinking you have done enough work already. By seeing yourself so clearly now, you will be able to go out in the world and use your willpower and newfound knowledge to overcome this thing plaguing you.

Do not fall for this trap. It is a self-help trap. I know because I went down this road and only repeated the same story again, got more beat up by my own self, harmed more people, and was left alone and trapped inside a never-ending cycle I could not escape on my own. If you have completed your inventory, good job; you have probably seen some uncomfortable things. And if, like me, you understand that you cannot escape ON YOUR OWN POWER, it is time to move on to the next step of admission. It is going to be much easier than you think.

Dear Divine Spirit, please set aside everything I think I know about myself, about my story, about my problem, and especially about you, Spirit, so that I may have an open mind and a new experience with myself, with my story, with my problem, and with you, Spirit. Please help me to see the truth. Please show me the truth about my powerlessness. Please show me the truth in this inventory. Amen.

A prayer of surrender:

Dear Divine Spirit, I offer my life to you to do with as you see fit. Take away my selfishness, take away my unmanageability, so that freedom from them will show others that I will help your power, love, and a way of life. May I do your will in everything that I do. Amen.

Increase your morning quiet time to fifteen minutes.

Chapter Four
Admission: No Man (or Woman) Is an Island

"The original, shimmering self gets buried so deep that most of us end up hardly living out of it at all. Instead, we live out all the other selves, which we are constantly putting on and taking off like coats and hats against the world's weather."
– Frederick Buechner.

"Your visions will become clear only when you can look into your own heart. Who looks outside, dreams; who looks inside, awakes." –
C.G. Jung

"You are only as sick as your secrets." –
Anonymous

The whole premise of this book is that you and I cannot change ourselves or these ingrained habits and behaviors on our own. We need something beyond ourselves to make these changes. While I knew that I needed something beyond myself, I was reluctant to share the more intimate details of my life. Why should you do this? The most important reason is that if you do not do this, you are more than likely always going to return to the pattern of behavior that got you where you were in the first place. You will not be able to just get over it and move on. I know this because that's what happened to me and others I know who have done this before. Over and over again, they tried to keep some of these private things to themselves and, almost without fail, returned back to the thing they were powerless over.

The other reason is that we cannot fully see ourselves, and especially those things that have become so habituated that it's like wearing an old set of pajamas. They are torn and frayed, but you have worn them for so long you cannot imagine getting a new pair. I could not see myself fully. I needed help from someone else as well as from the Source. The admission step was the way to do that. It was the first step toward true inner peace and contentment.

No man or woman is an island. We are incredibly social creatures and need people in our lives. We need community, family, and companionship. We do not operate or live in a vacuum, even though I have believed that in the past. I thought that no one knew how I was living or that my behavior did not affect other people, but that was not true.

I wanted to be able to look at these things I had written down, chew on them, learn from them, and move on. But that's *self*-help. And as we know, self-help sucks. I needed to go further. I needed to tell someone what I was doing (and what I've done). After all, if I am unwilling to talk about myself with another person, then the only person holding me accountable is *me. (*And that's *self*-help!) That is not where I want to be. I wanted freedom. I tried to stop doing what I was doing. What I had to do was swallow my pride, ask to have my ego set aside, and put down my armor and trust another human being with all the stuff I had been doing.

In my experience, the listener's role is first and foremost to be of service to the person reading the inventory. Listeners are not there as therapists, priests, or judges, though it can be meaningful when they can point out patterns and keep us from getting too sucked up in our stories. Listeners can keep us on track, point out the things we may not notice, and remind us we are not alone in our powerlessness by perhaps relating a story of their own.

This exercise is not a religious confession. Get rid of that idea. We are not confessing our "sins." You may call them whatever you like, but I find that such language relies too much on context and can mean different things depending on who's listening. So, if you want to use that word for your exercise, be my guest. I prefer "heaviness." I needed (and wanted) to get rid of the heavy things in my heart. I kept going against my morals and values, making the same mistakes repeatedly, and I was sick of it. My heaviness was making me sick, and I needed to get it off my chest. I needed to tell someone else what I had been doing in order for this Power to enter my heart in a meaningful way.

I think there is a spiritual significance to reading our heaviness aloud and hearing it read to you. It takes vulnerability and humility to tell someone your dirty laundry out loud. Having a partner to do this exercise with where you both read to each other creates an environment of trust, honesty and vulnerability.

The next question was: Who do I ask to do this admission exercise with me? I had plenty of friends who would be willing to do this, but willingness isn't enough. It was essential to do it with someone who would understand what I was trying to do, who would be gentle yet firm and keep me on track. I found someone to do this work with me, and we read our admissions to each other. We each took a day to read all the stuff we had written down. That way, we were on an equal playing field. There was no judge, jury, or executioner—just two people who wanted to get the things that had been plaguing them off their plate.

Later in the book, we talk about letting go of the stories. We tell ourselves stories all day long. We attach meaning to things without knowing what those things *really* mean or why people do them. We create stories and fill in the blanks. Saying to myself that people did something for a specific reason or how people think are all stories that I really do not know are true. I create resentments and fears about these stories. None of them have ever been true. I needed to not get caught up in a story about why people do what they do or attach meaning to what I thought they did, because I should only look at myself here. I can only stick to the facts without veering off into the never-ending spiral of the story. When listening to someone else read their inventory, as kindly and gently as possible, help them stick to the facts and do not let them get lost in the story.

We get down to business, and each takes a turn at reading this inventory to the other person. We are gentle and kind yet firm when listening and asking questions for clarification or to help them move out of the story and into the facts. Hold nothing back, and you will feel like a new person—like coming up for air after holding your breath for too long.

After you finish, find a place to be quiet for a while, about an hour or two. The purpose of this quiet time is to spend some time reflecting on what you just shared. It is also to have some time to get closer to God and, in my case, nature. I like walking in the woods. Take the time to consider what it is in this writing about yourself that you do not like about your behavior anymore. What is it that you no longer want to do any longer? What are your faults that you want to be removed?

I have gone against myself and my principles repeatedly. What are the flaws in my makeup that are eating me for breakfast? Toward the end of my walk, I have a heart-to-heart talk with the Power, the Universe, the Spirit of the Forest I am in. I tell it precisely what it is in myself that I no longer want to be doing. I say it without judgment, without pleading or begging, and ask the Power to give me the will to let go of these behaviors. I ask it to remove everything that stands in the way of me being useful and helpful and blocks me from the people in this world and my life.

I must be willing to put in some effort here, of course. Transformation is not a one-way street. *Self*-help sucks, but we are not made valiant without any action on our part. We must be willing to let go of certain things in ourselves, even if they feel good, and ask the Power to change us, to remove the obstacles in our path (and personality). By telling someone else everything in your inventory, you will have admitted out loud the very things you want God to remove, that which stands in the way of your progress and hinders your spiritual growth. You must also ask for the strength to do whatever is needed to be closer to it–and where and with whom you must make amends.

Dear Divine Spirit, please set aside everything I think I know about myself, about my story, about my problem, and especially about you, Spirit, so that I may have an open mind and a new experience with myself, with my story, with my problem, and with you, Spirit. Please help me to see the truth. Please show me the truth about my powerlessness. Please show me the truth about my faults. Amen.

Dear Divine Spirit, I offer my life to you to do with as you see fit. Take away my selfishness, take away my unmanageability, so that freedom from them will show others that I will help your power, love, and a way of life. May I do your will in everything that I do. Amen.

A prayer of admission:

Dear Divine Spirit, I come to you after this inventory with an open heart and open mind. There are some things in myself that no longer serve me or the people in my life. Above all, I want to be rid of them. Please remove them from me and make me into the person I so desire to be. Grant me the power to go out from here to do your bidding. Amen.

Increase your morning quiet time to eighteen minutes.

Chapter Five
Restitution: Repairing the Harm

"Mistakes are always forgivable if one has the courage to admit them." – Bruce Lee

"It is the highest form of self-respect to admit our errors and mistakes and make amends for them. To make a mistake is only an error in judgment, but to adhere to it when it is discovered shows infirmity of character."
– Dale Turner

The subtitle of this book is *The Anti-Self-Help Guide to Inner Peace and Contentment*. There is a guarantee with that phrase: you will achieve inner peace and contentment if you follow the steps in this guide. It will absolutely change your life. Possibly in the beginning, like me, you were only hoping to be free of the thing in your life that has been plaguing you. What I am here to tell you is that it is much more than that. It is the ability to go anywhere and not be afraid, to answer the phone no matter who calls, to have freedom from fear, and to have a consistent sense of well-being and satisfaction that does not fade as your life's circumstances change, to experience true humility. These are the things that come with this process. What stands in your way are the harms that you have caused people in your life. The deeper you are willing to go here, the freer you can be.

I believed that I only had to make amends based on my current situation or, if you will, the thing which brought me to my knees in the first place. I found it was necessary to go further if I wanted peace.

I spent a lot of years revolving in and out of the twelve-step program. I would clean up physically, get back into society, and start to rebuild my life. Then I'd make it to the amends step and quit. This time was different, though; the idea of going back to where I was made me feel so uncomfortable that it began to feel like a threat. I could not fathom returning to powerlessness, so I asked my Higher Power for help making amends to the people in my life whom I had hurt.

Restitution is a vital part of doing the work; it has to be done. If you truly want long-lasting change and a release from the patterns in your life, you must do something different.

The amends process did that for me. Once I made amends, a personality change occurred in me that was impossible to create on my own. I had tried therapy, self-help, and medication, and every effort that I had attempted failed and I always returned to what I was before—only worse. It also, in many ways, removed my fear of other people. I no longer had to be afraid to answer the phone or worry about who I would run into at the store. I could go anywhere and not be scared. The same goes for monetary amends.

My experience is that if I was unwilling to pay the money I owed, I was always afraid about money and never felt like I had enough. Once I made even just a few initial payments, I began to lose my fear. I felt as though I always had enough—not to mention the benefit of increasing my credit score. In the twelve-step movement, the ninth step says, "We made direct amends to such people wherever possible, except when to do so would injure them or others." How do we do that, and what does it entail?

First, stop being sorry. Sorry never fixed anything. I've found that most of the time, feeling sorry is an excuse to keep doing the same shit to people. The "hurt, apologize, repeat" cycle does little more than make everyone so sick of your shit that they walk out of your life and never say a word about it. Most people will just walk away. Really. I know because I've lived it. That's why this restitution step is so essential. Without it, there's no transformation. If I am not willing to talk to people about how I have treated them and make amends, I will continue to hurt others. They will continue to leave, and I will never have any meaningful, vulnerable relationships in my life. A well-meaning guru once asked me, "How free do you want to be?" I think that question applies here. How badly did I want to stop doing what I was doing? Did I want it bad enough to go through with making amends to those I'd wronged, the step that I kept avoiding? How badly do you want it? Because without restitution, there can be no transformation.

Here is the process I followed. I encourage you to do it too. I got out my notebook and asked the Power to show me who I needed to make amends to. Who in my life had I hurt? Write truthfully; there's no room for ambiguity here. Once I get those names down, each person gets a blank sheet of paper, and I write a prayer at the top of the page for God to enable me to see the truth for each person that comes up on this list.

What do we mean when we talk about harm? What are some ways that we harm people, and what exactly does it mean to make amends? The word harm means to damage or injure physically, to cause harm, which seems redundant, but that's the definition. Below I list all the areas to look at for each person on my list.

There are five categories:

Physical: Did you hurt them physically in some way?

Mental: Mental harm is where I make an agreement to do something and do not follow through with my commitment to do what I said I would do.

Emotional: Did I break their heart in some way?

Spiritual: Spiritual harm is where I degrade someone's spirit, such as always making comments about them or people "like them."

Financial: Do I owe them or anyone any money? Did I borrow something I did not give back? Did I waste time at my job, doing my own thing on my employer's dime? How's my credit report? Is there anything on there that I can clean up or repay?

Take each piece of paper, write down the name at the top of the page, write your prayer, and make your list of categories on the left-hand side. Along with each one, write down the harm you believe you've caused. Be specific.

As in the case of me flirting with other women in front of my wife, I was inflicting emotional, spiritual, and mental harm. I had mentally harmed her by going against my agreement to exemplify certain behaviors as a husband, I hurt her emotionally by flirting with other women, and I degraded her spiritually by doing so in front of her. Once I have finished the list and have prayed and meditated on it, what do I do now?

If I drive my car into your yard and run over your fence and break it, not only do I need to admit that I drove into the yard and broke it, but I also need to mend the fence. It is not good enough to merely change our behavior; we must admit our wrong and acknowledge our harm. How we do that can take many forms, such as in person, in writing, or over the phone, but in the end, it is up to you and your Higher Power how you approach each person. The benefit of a face-to-face conversation is that you get to look the person in the eye and can see and hear how you affected them. Writing is a good approach for people whom you cannot see for some reason or another. I have done it over the phone on a few occasions, and while it did not feel the same as doing it in person, sometimes it is the best way to go.

When I approach someone in person or over the phone, I have found it helpful to stay concise:

I was wrong in how I treated you when I was flirting with those women in front of you, you did not deserve to be treated that way, and I regret doing it. Please forgive me for how I acted. I will not do that again. Would you like to talk to me about how this made you feel?

Then wait. Listen and do not interrupt. When the other person has said all they want to, let them know you appreciate their honesty and acknowledge their perspective:

Thank you for sharing that with me. I appreciate it. I know that would not have made me feel very good, and I love you and appreciate you listening.

You can modify this approach to suit your coworkers, friends, or family members—and while I probably would not tell the person at my job that I love them, I can admit I was wrong in how I spoke to them or treated them. Then it is our job, as the person making amends, to change our behavior with God's help.

Speaking for myself, I may need to ask every day for help to change. I mean, I got some juice out of flirting with these women. It made me feel good, almost like a drug! But once I talked with my wife about it and saw the look on her face and put myself in her shoes for a minute, I knew that I would be angry, hurt, and jealous if she acted that way. Her pain outweighed my desire for a feel-good hit. So, I asked God for the strength to stop and made my amends to my wife. Mostly, except for a couple of hiccups, I have stayed true to that and do not flirt with other women (unless they are senior citizens and flirt with me first).

Self-help really sucks here because our egos will try to convince us that we do not need to do this step, that this whole amends thing is going too far, that we can just stop being an asshole and don't have to talk to anyone about it. We will look to as many people as possible to sign on to this belief system and continue to stay precisely where we are. That's what your ego wants—and if you listen, you will get worse. You will continue to get sicker and sicker and more and more dependent on your powerless behavior. I know that because I've lived it. The only way is to slide down. Your ego will convince you that it is better to just walk away or make some noncommittal comment about being sorry or just letting bygones be bygones. But I am telling you to not fall for that shit. It is a lie, a trick, nothing but a dog and pony show. Listen to "Frannie," who has done the same thing as me, talk about her amends process.

I have gone out and made reparations to those I harmed.

This was very difficult at first but has become a matter of practice. It wasn't easy before, and it still is not easy. This is due to my pride. Knowing that it is necessary to maintain my sobriety and emotional balance, I can now quickly go from defending my harm to seeing the necessity of repairing the harm. I will make up a hundred reasons to not do this. What I do know is that I need my sponsor's guidance to do this. Some apologies I want to make have the wrong motives behind them. I may say things that could cause more anger and harm to the person, so words are carefully chosen. I have made this mistake and had to apologize for the apology. I need my Higher Power to give me proper humility and courage. The freedom this process has given me is the most tangible part of the program. Years of fear and the feeling of carrying a heavy burden are gone. I have a general feeling of serenity and closeness to God."

In my experience, financial amends are the most challenging. But I also do not believe I could have felt the way I do today—unafraid about money, where it will come from, or not having enough—without making monetary amends. It certainly taught me the most, and it completely rewrote my relationship with money. I now know I will always be taken care of and that my actual dependence is on my Higher Power, not money. I could not have gotten here from where I was if I chose to ignore my financial life.

I started with a credit report and a brain dump of who I believed I owed money to. I owed student loan debt, personal debt, and credit card debt. I had borrowed money I had not paid back and lived paycheck to paycheck with hardly any money in savings. Unsurprisingly, I almost always ran out of money before the next check came and was afraid I would not have enough.

So I'd deprive myself of even necessary items like new underwear or socks because of my fear of running out of money.

I would eat ramen when I could have been eating filet mignon, all based on my fear. The longer I avoided the money issue and what I owed, the more afraid I was, the more I tried to hoard, and the more broke I got. I could not get out of the spiral of my fear and do something to change it on my own, I was trapped by my own self-help program, and it was not working.

So, I asked the Power to change my story about money, change my beliefs about money, and change my relationship with it. On the back of American paper currency, near the top of the bill, is a banner that says "In God We Trust." It does not say in money we trust, or in America we trust, or in ourselves we trust. It says in God we trust. I had to ask for that trust and follow through with some action contrary to my fear.

Then I started paying back *their* money. It is not mine if I owe it to them; it is theirs—and if the debt is paid, it's God's money, not mine. Money is a tool meant to be used for good, to give back, and to help. The exciting thing is that once I started paying back what I owed, my fear began to disappear. Suddenly, I started having leftover money at the end of the pay cycle. I began to go out to eat a little more. I bought things when I needed them and began to rely on this Power to provide for me. Which it always has. As I understand it, the law of the Universe is that if you tell the Universe that you do not have enough, you will not have enough. If you say to the Universe that you have enough, you will always have enough.

Now, I no longer owe anyone anything from the past. I am willing to carry some debt, such as our house, a car payment, and the current bills required for our life such as cell phones, insurance, and things like that, but nothing is plaguing me financially. I want that same freedom for you.

Get some help if you need it. If you are over your head in credit card debt, get some credit counseling and make the payments. Always make the payments. Ask people who had gone before you on the path what they did to clean up their financial lives. Most anyone approached in this way will be happy to help. It is our job to be able to be of service to the people in our lives.

When it comes to making amends, I believe the further we are willing to go here, the better we will get. I had to be ready to approach everyone I could and mend the fences I had broken (some fences I had to replace entirely). But I found that the more I was willing to admit my wrongs, the more human I became. I believe this holds true for everyone. We get to be free.

For this step, write a list of people and institutions you believe you have harmed and what you think your financial harms are. Use a credit report to identify any financial issues you may be unaware of. Each person gets a blank piece of paper. Write a prayer at the top of the page that you are shown the truth. For each person, list the categories of harm and write what you believe the injury was.

Financial: Do I owe them money?

Emotional: Have I broken their heart or said something that hurt them?

Mental: Did I make an agreement that I did not keep, even an unspoken one?

Spiritual: Have I degraded their spirit?
Physical: Did I hurt them physically?

Begin the prayer practice below, consistently asking your Higher Power to put these people in your path. In my experience, it will be obvious who you are to approach. Admit your wrongs, ask for forgiveness, express regret, and assure them that you will do your best not to repeat that behavior in the future. Make sure no one else will be harmed by the amends you are making. This is not about being sorry; it is about righting your wrongs. As a result of this step, you will gain peace of mind and increased self-worth, have better relationships with people, have fewer regrets, and develop a deeper relationship with your Higher Power.

Dear Divine Spirit, please set aside everything I think I know about myself, about my story, about my problem, and especially about you, Spirit, so that I may have an open mind and a new experience with myself, with my story, with my problem, and with you, Spirit. Please help me to see the truth. Amen.

A prayer of surrender:

Dear Divine Spirit, I offer my life to you to do with as you see fit. Take away my selfishness, take away my unmanageability, so that freedom from them will show others that I will help your power, your love, and a way of life. May I do your will in everything that I do. Amen.

A prayer for amends:

God, please give me the strength and opportunity to repair the damage I have caused in my life. Give me the power to make amends to the people in my life that I have harmed. Show me where you would have me go to be the person I am intended to be. Give me the words to say so that I cause no further injury. Give me the strength to do the right thing, no matter what that may be. Amen.

Increase your morning quiet time to twenty minutes of daily meditation.

Chapter Six
Service: You Got to Give It Away, Man

"What is the essence of life? To serve others and to do good." – Aristotle

"Service to others is the rent you pay for your room here on Earth." – Muhammad Ali

The greatest gift in my life came to me while I was in the service to others. I met my wife while volunteering at our local homeless shelter, and because we gave of our most valuable asset, our time, our lives have become enriched and full. Whenever I feel down or need a mental kick in the butt, I go over to the local homeless shelter and give my time. Every time I walk away from there, I feel immense gratitude for being alive, for really not having one single problem in my life, and knowing that we are all connected by the Source and all the same at our cellular level. This last step is about giving of ourselves, looking for and finding the opportunity to pass along what you have learned from these steps, committing to your version of a Higher Power and to yourself that if anyone shows up in your life that needs your help, you'll claim that responsibility. The returns you get from serving others are far greater than any other feeling. Trust me.

The whole twelve-step program can be summarized into the six steps used before Bill Wilson, who was one of the co-founders of Alcoholics Anonymous. had his revelation to make it into twelve. They were:

Step One: Admit hopelessness.

Step Two: Get honest with yourself.

Step Three: Get honest with another.

Step Four: Made amends.

Step Five: Help others without demand.

Step Six: Pray to God as you understand him.

Once I admitted that I cannot do things on

my own, I had to find a Power by which I could live who could give me the strength to do what was needed. Part of forming the relationship necessary to that Power requires clearing away what has blocked me from it and finding the things that connect me to it. The thing that has consistently kept me connected is being of service to others. In the twelve-step program, that looks like sponsorship and showing others what you have done to help them do their own work. Since our process here is not part of a twelve-step program, and you may or may not want to join one, how can you find the opportunity to help others with this work?

One of my favorite tenets of the twelve-step movement is that after you have your spiritual experience—or maybe more accurately, while you are rebuilding your life—your job is to help others with the same affliction experience the twelve-step process. Of course, Bill Wilson did not come up with this idea himself. Many movements used this principle before Alcoholics Anonymous adopted it. The Washingtonians, the Oxford Group, and most religions are founded on helping others adopt their principles.

The great thing here is we are not on a membership drive. We are not trying to get members, nor are we collecting dues or trickle-down financial effects from helping people do this. But I found that showing other people how to find their own brand of help was the most effective way to avoid repeating my mistakes. That is the nice thing about twelve-step meetings: most people are there for the same thing. They have some overshadowing problem in their life that they became powerless over and admit they needed help. By going into a social environment where you are surrounded by people who have been where you have been and done the things you have done, you finally feel understood—and it's an incredible feeling to talk about the way you were living and see everyone around you nod their head in identification because they have all done the same thing too.

If you do not have this community in your life, where can you find people to help? I suggest volunteering at the homeless shelter, looking for people online, volunteering at the animal shelter, or being of service in an online community that revolves around helping others in some kind of way. What you put out into the Universe, it sends back to you exponentially. If your attitude is one of contribution, people will start showing up in your life seemingly out of nowhere. A coworker suddenly brings up their personal problems, which sound an awful lot like what you were struggling with—yes, that will start to happen. These people will show up in your life because they need you to share your experience with them. They need to know they are not alone.

There's one exception to what you can share. Most people, including me, must meet God alone. No one can create an experience for another person, nor can they make it happen to them. Each person must have their own "dark night of the soul," as St. John of the Cross called it in his poem by the same name. Each of us has to arrive at that place on our own, that moment where we finally ask some hard questions.

When they start to ask those questions, it is

your job to share what you have done. It is not your job to tell other people how to live, spend their money, or manage their relationships, but sharing your experience is valuable. So if you have found your own powerlessness with something in your life, share it with people. It's counterculture to do this kind of thing as the messaging in this world is to be strong and an achiever, to get the accolades and awards, and "never let 'em see you sweat." But is that true for any of us? I don't think so. Telling the truth is more valuable, especially to someone who needs to hear it.

These people will start showing up in your life. They will have the same stuff as you too— you'll spot it a mile away. Make yourself available, but don't be overbearing. Most people like chocolate, even vegans like chocolate if it is vegan, but no one likes it shoved down their throat. Invite, don't force. And in the meantime, let the way you live speak for you.

We live the principles we have learned, which morphs into a daily practice and way of life. We keep our spirit open to those we can help along the way. In my case, it is important to me to give back to my community, so volunteering at the local homeless shelter is where I feel the most connected and helpful. Self-help sucks; other people's help does not. The more I give back to this world, the more I get back in return. It is easy to write a check and put it in the mail—which you really should do if you feel so inclined—but our time is the most precious commodity that we have. It is where we will meet our fellows, out on the path, walking side by side as we help one another shoulder each other's burdens. Take one step at a time. Listen to what another person has to say about helping others:

Over time I start thinking and behaving differently. I begin to think about helping other people instead of being consumed by my anger and fear. I smile more, reconnect with friends, begin singing instead of screaming in the car. I genuinely want to know how your day is going instead of constantly bitching about mine. I show up for people in small or large ways. I bring a friend's favorite sandwich to her while she's in the hospital. I watch a mom with four small kids keep it together while waiting an hour for dinner. I tell her what a great job she's doing. I focus on what I can bring to the world around me instead of how I can control the world around me.

If you have done the work in this book and it has helped you in some way, show someone else what you did and share with them your story of transformation. Give it away for fun and for free, go out into the world and help every person you can. Repay the money you owe and repair the relationships you can; you will be free. Find a Higher Power and cultivate a relationship with it to the best of your ability. Continue to check in with yourself regularly and examine your life. Carefully watch for when irritation and judgment start to creep back in, and when they do (and they will), do this work all over again. There is always something worth looking at further.

Self-help sucks, but there are things we can do to help ourselves. With the help of a Power greater than myself, I can make an effort to change—but I have to do the work. I must decide myself and ask that I am given the will to do what needs to get done and do it. What happens as a result is not up to me; I do not control the Universe.

The next chapter is devoted to the daily life that I intend to live and the tools I use each day to not go back to what I was before.

When I last did this work, I did it with a partner. We read to each other and shared the things that came out of each rung in the ladder. I had done it before and knew that if I did not show someone else how to do it, I would forget everything I had seen about myself. I would forget the pain I had caused myself and other people and, again, be relying on *self*-help—and as we know, *self*-help sucks.

Dear Divine Spirit, as I go out into this day, show me who I can help and put into my path whomever I can be of the most service to. Let me have this in everything I do. Show me the way of patience, tolerance, and love. Amen

Prayer and meditation is now at 20 mins.

Chapter Seven
The Way to Inner Peace

"You should sit in meditation for twenty minutes every day unless you are too busy; then you should sit for an hour." – Zen Proverb

In 2009, I married a woman who did not like or want children, even though I had always wanted them. After three months of being married, she told me what I already knew to be the truth. She did not want children, never had, and marrying me (and my incessant demands that we start having kids right away) further clarified this truth. I had already known how she felt but did not listen, and we went ahead and married anyway.

On top of that, I was rarely home. My job demanded that I be away from my new home and my new wife all the time. I worked nights, weekends, holidays, and typically could not (or would not) show up for her completely or consistently. I was always looking at pornography and doing what men do when looking at pornography (unless they are a porno film critic, which I am sure is out there). I was unhappy, and I did not know it. Nor was I willing to stop for one minute and look at it or check in with my feelings to ask myself if I was content and living by the principles I had set down in my life. None of this was her fault. It was me.

One winter day in February, I drove with my mountain bike about two hours away to meet a group of mountain bikers to do some winter riding where the trails were dry. I had never met these guys before but had hooked up with them over a meetup website for mountain bike enthusiasts.

We rode around this beautiful northern New Mexico landscape with amazing views and a nice trail system that was not very challenging but was fun, nonetheless. We were on our way back to the trailhead when the group found a great spot for doing jumps on the mountain bike. All of us lined up to do this jump. I was somewhere in the middle of the line and, though my first time through was fun, I didn't perform as well as I'd wanted. So I got back in line to attempt the jump again, but decided this time I would give it everything I had and go as fast as I could to really get some air and impress these guys whom I had never met before.

I walked my bike up to the starting point, and suddenly, I had this thought that I didn't need to do this, that I should just quit right now and forget what I had planned. I completely disregarded those thoughts and got on my bike and hammered, and I mean *hammered,* on the pedals to fly toward this jump. The wind blew through the vents of the helmet, my hands were glued to the handlebars, my legs pumped with all they had. My speed was reckless and dangerous. I hit the jump, but the bike landed on its front tire first. I got thrown over the handlebars and slammed into the frozen ground right on my head, cracking the helmet in several different places. I lay on the dirt with electricity zapping through my arms, my hands, and my neck. The other guys helped me up, and I rode my bike back to the car. They helped me load everything up, and I began the two-hour drive back home.

I was sweating, disorientated, and knew something was wrong. I called my wife and told her I had wrecked the bike and was going to urgent care because I was sure that I had just tweaked my neck or something, and they could just somehow fix it. I walked into the urgent care facility, which was right next door to the hospital, and told them the story. They called an ambulance to take me next door to the hospital, *a hundred feet away*. In the emergency room, the doctors sent me for a CAT scan and an MRI. I was told I had broken my C5 and C6 vertebrae and either needed a fusion or disc replacement right away. That meant I'd be flown or driven down to the University of New Mexico hospital in Albuquerque, where the chief neurosurgeon was already there to perform the surgery.

After it was done, I woke up in my hospital room all alone. One of the doctors came in to ask me how I was feeling and proceeded to tell me that I was two millimeters away from being a paraplegic, that I had come within the height of two pennies stacked together to never walking again! As soon as he left, I was overcome with the realization that out there in the desert, on that frozen hard ground, I was caught by an enormous hand that carried me in its embrace all the way back, even as I drove with a broken neck for two hours, most likely in shock.

I also had the sudden realization and rush of emotion that right next to our world is an invisible one that connects all of us, that there is a Power that made the primordial building blocks of the Universe—and if it could catch me and get me to where I lay in that ICU hospital bed, it had my attention. I knew intuitively that this Power is always accessible and available to us and was overcome with a feeling of peace, serenity, and love for everyone. That morning, I told the Power that I would sit with it every day, that I would not miss a single one, and I dedicated my life to it. Since that day, I can count on one hand the number of days I have missed sitting with that Power. The consistency of our "meetings" has absolutely changed my life.

Very shortly afterward, my wife and I decided that we had far too different goalposts in our life as I could not let go of wanting a child. We divorced amicably and civilly, and I genuinely care for her and wish her happiness and a successful life. And so it was just the Power and me.

Despite the physical pain of my recovery and the emotional pain of my breakup, I did not miss a day—not one. I sat with the Power every morning, first in silence and then in connectedness as my practice developed.

Before then, I had always desired constant spiritual connectedness but did not have a consistent spiritual practice. Meditation, or even the idea of sitting quietly with my thoughts, was extremely difficult. I had a hectic mind and was ruled by my thoughts and emotions. I constantly reacted to other people and what I thought they were thinking. I responded to how I felt about something instead of the thing itself. But through my experience with my broken neck, where I genuinely felt an invisible force right beside me, I felt a love for my fellow man that I had never felt before and understood did not come from me. I felt it and made the commitment out loud to sit with it. But then I couldn't help but wonder, *Now, what the heck am I going to do?*

Meditation can be intimidating if you've never done it before. I had all kinds of ideas (stories) about what meditation is and what it's not. Even though I had minimal experience with it and had only done it sporadically and inconsistently, I believed that I was not supposed to think. My mind was supposed to be a blank slate. I was supposed to be inspired all the time and walk out into the world as a spiritually enlightened being who shined my light on everyone I met and levitated because I was so spiritual. I thought I had to be in a quiet monk's cell sequestered from the rest of the world and have a gong ring its vibrating soul sound into my bones to meditate. I thought I had to sit in the correct position, on the right pillow, with my head a certain way. All these ideas were wrong, and even though some of them had a thread of possibility, none of them have been my experience. To get past the stories or old beliefs, first I had to have an experience. I had to start doing it, and since I did not know how, I had to get some help from somewhere else. *Self*-help sucks!

Fortunately, there is magic in making a start. Making the decision to sit down every day opened a magic portal that accessed a power I did not possess on my own. Once I made this decision and got started, I found a practice called Centering Prayer. Here is what I did to start and what I do now.

1. Choose a sacred word as the symbol of your intention to consent to God's presence and action within.
2. Sitting comfortably and with eyes closed, settle briefly and silently introduce the sacred word as the symbol of your consent to God's presence and action within.
3. When you become aware of thoughts, return ever so gently to the sacred word.
4. At the end of the prayer period, remain in silence with eyes closed for a couple of minutes.

I started by praying and asking for a sacred word or phrase that came from my heart. Some examples of these may be *Love, God, Christ, Presence, Mother, Divine Mother, Allah, Jeshua, Kindness*, or what comes to you from inside of you. It is only a symbol–think of it like a key that unlocks the door to the Power that creates and sustains life, the twenty-one grams of the soul, or if you prefer, the Power that connects us all.

The word is the key to your acknowledgment that something bigger than you out there has energy, and that is all things that you cannot control or produce on your own. If you doubt that, go out into your backyard and focus your energy on making the plants and flowers in your yard bloom and grow. I'm serious. Really concentrate. I'll be here when you are done. You will have made nothing grow or blossom; you'll just need a nap. That Power, the one you *don't* have, is the one I am talking about. Your word is the key to open the mental door to that Power.

Next, find a comfortable place to sit down. I sit on the couch. You figure out what works for you and your body. Just pick a spot and start doing it. Set a timer for five minutes. If you feel like you can do longer, that is cool; I was so wound up that five minutes was all I could do to start.

Start by saying your word or phrase. As you sit, your thoughts come and go like passing clouds, so to speak. Do not worry about them, do not attach meaning; just let them pass if you can. There should be no effort on your part to control what is happening or the thoughts as they come or not, or even what they're about. When you grab onto an idea or start to tell a story about one of your thoughts, say your word quietly in your mind until the thought goes its own way.

Here's an example. Let's say that during your quiet time you have the thought that you should pick up some flowers for your partner. If the thought stops there, that is just a thought—do not worry about it. But if your mind keeps going *"Well, I will get pink roses, and I will go to this flower shop, and she will be so surprised,"* blah, blah blah, that is when you should say your word or phrase in your mind, gently until that story goes away. Do this the entire time of your meditation, and after the timer goes off, gently repeat your word or phrase and go about your day. I finish my meditation with a prayer to be shown who I can help today. I ask to be given the ability to help them, to listen to my intuition, and be shown all through the day where I am supposed to go and what I am supposed to do. Here is an example from another person:

What I need is to stop fighting life, accept circumstances and people, and trust something bigger than myself to take care of me. Because my anger comes from fear, I choose to trust something which makes me feel safe no matter what happens in my life. Something bigger than me can be anything I feel safe with: a mountain, the ocean, the starry night sky, a place, a feeling, or a thought. With practice, I can conjure up the place I feel safe absolutely anytime, anywhere. I live in a landlocked state. The closest ocean is more than an hour's flight away. Right now, I close my eyes and can hear the waves running ashore, feel the sand indent under my feet. I can feel the salty water pushing against my legs, then my waist, and the energy it takes to swim out past the surf. I love the weightlessness and quiet of floating in the ocean.

When I find myself caught up in a story that keeps going on and on in my head, I take a breath and say my word or phrase. I pray to be reminded that I am not in charge of this world, ask to be shown my next step, and for freedom from my selfishness. It is incredible how often I slip into the trap of my desires trying to run the show.

And that's it. That's the foundation of your practice. Now you just have to be consistent and add time when you're ready. I built from five minutes to ten minutes to fifteen minutes to twenty minutes to thirty minutes. Thirty was a little too much for me and our household, so I settled on twenty-five.

Let me tell you a story. When my wife Alicia and I started dating, I asked her to join me in my morning meditation. Her spiritual and religious beliefs are very different from mine. Still, I also knew that every single one of my relationships had never made it past the point of infatuation—and when that excitement fizzles, it's like a firework show the day after a rain. All that's left are the hollow shells of the firing chambers and ashes. I did not want that anymore and decided that if I was trying to live this life spiritually, why not give it all by asking it to guide my life. And truth be told, all of the couples I have seen that have had longevity and sustained attractiveness in their relationship have some kind of spiritual life together, or each has their own spiritual life that meets somewhere in the middle of all of it. To this day, we both have our own spiritual practice, and it has been the glue that has kept us together in tough times. I am grateful I had the courage to ask her. It is the most intimate thing to pray together and have each other's happiness in mind.

Our Hazel is a toddler now. She is a high-energy, talkative child. One morning I was sitting in bed doing my meditation when in popped Hazel. She started climbing all over me and chatting up a storm, just being a three-year-old little girl. I found myself getting irritated that she was distracting me and interrupting my time. I could feel my heart rate increasing, feel the heat climbing to my face, and I started to say something snappy at her like, "Daddy is trying to have quiet time, Hazel.

Can you be quiet?" Then out of nowhere–actually, no, I do not believe it was out of nowhere–I got this overpowering sense that this little girl was how my Higher Power was showing me that I am loved. All the crawling over me and chatting was my Higher Power's way of saying *I love you*. So, from there on out, if my daughter wants to climb all over me when I am meditating, I think of it as a good thing. The well-known author and meditative Alan Watts said if you can't meditate in a boiler room, then you can't meditate.

In my experience, it's not helpful to "grade" your time with your Higher Power. I kept labeling my meditation time as good or bad. If I had a morning where my mind was busy and active, it was a bad meditation. And if I had a morning where my mind was quieter, I labeled it a good one. As I continued my practice–and yes, there is a reason it is called practice–the realization came to me that the true benefit of my meditation was not when I sat in the morning but when its effects came to me during my day. I found myself calmer when, in the past, I had been reacting to everything. I used to respond to things based on my belief whether they were good or bad. Now, my emotional state is no longer like a roller coaster. I began to have much more equanimity, reacting less and having a more level sense of well-being regardless of what was happening around me.

No matter how much I had tried in the past, I could not and still cannot produce this effect myself. It is only through the cultivation of my spiritual life that this growth came about. I did not create it or envision it. It just happened.

The other thing that happened is that I became nicer. I have always been abrupt and insensitive. I would show no regard for what kind of situation I was in or what kind of people I was surrounded by. I'd just make inappropriate comments to see what kind of reaction I'd get. Now, when the urge to spurt out some random inappropriate comment comes to my mind, I have been given the discernment to pause and the ability to keep my mouth shut. I began to practice mindful speech, asking myself before I blurt out something or give someone advice they didn't ask for in the first place: *Is it true? Is it necessary? Is it kind or loving? Does it need to be said now?*

In the next chapter, I will talk about my rules for living, but the point is that this experience with my Higher Power happened *to me*; I did not make it happen. I have made solemn oaths and commitments to change for most of my life and have had many heartfelt discussions about needing and wanting to change. Still, I was never able to pull it off on my own. Why? Because *self*-help sucks, right? Right.

As my practice has grown, I've also added an evening check-in with my Higher Power. I treat it as a routine inventory at the end of the day in which I review my thoughts, actions, and potential harms for the day or close to it. I made a little notebook with questions to answer at the end of the day, and I write them down, so I know what needs to be worked on tomorrow. *Was I angry?* Which means any kind of irritation or disturbance to the mind in this way at all. *Was I selfish? Was I afraid?* Mostly of not getting what I want or losing what I have. Also, of not being good enough. *Was I dishonest? Do I owe an apology to someone for something I said or did?*

There is nothing too "small" to explore. What I might think is the most minor thing in the world might have the potential to completely blow up my life—so I want to make sure I don't miss it. I am always tuned into myself with the understanding that everything I feel is filtering through me. *Everything.* I can make every single interaction and nuance about me. My wife can have a particular look on her face, and I will ask her, "Why are you angry at me?" To which she says, "I only had to burp!" I made that look about me—and I do that with almost everything.

It should come as no surprise then that I ask these questions at the end of the day. The answer is rarely, if ever, no. I've found that if you sense enough to ask the question, the answer won't surprise you.

I continue with my questions: *Did I adhere to mindful speech today? What did I not accomplish today? What is my plan for tomorrow?* At the end of my inventory, I say a prayer, thanking the

Universe for my life, family, and health. I ask for forgiveness for anyone and for myself for my mistakes, realizing that my Power does not judge me, even though I certainly judge myself. I pray for my family, and I pray for this world. I slip off into the land of Nod and dream the dreams sent to me from above. Your practice may look entirely different, but I encourage you to find one that works for you—oh, and don't take yourself too seriously while you do it. Perfectionism and meditation do not mix well.

I have a practice, which I practice. It is only practice, so it's okay to screw up. There is no perfect. It does not exist; it has never existed on the human plane, and it never will. There is no try. There is only do or do not do. That is it.

Once I stopped worrying about doing it "right," I found it easier to meditate. And I stopped worrying about what other people thought. I realized *they were not thinking about me at all*. That no one was keeping score except for me, and all of my "failures" really only made me human, and I had flaws just like everyone else. It took away the pressure to attempt to be perfect or have a perfect spiritual practice. I just have a practice. It lays an outline for me to follow on a day-by-day basis, and it has produced a sense of contentment and equanimity that I never experienced before. None of those things happened because of me; they came from my Higher Power. All I do is show up every day—that's my job.

There are days, though, that I skip my evening review. I tell myself I don't need to, or I'm too tired, or I don't have anything to write about, and I just don't do it; one time, I skipped my reviews for a month! By the end of the month, I noticed that things were slipping out of my mouth that I did not want to slip out of my mouth. So, I asked the Power for some help and started practicing again. I will never be a spiritual guru, nor do I want to be; that is far too much work. But showing up? That I can do. I have permission to be human, to not be perfect, to be able to make mistakes and learn from them. I may stumble and slide back, or I may open my mouth again at some extremely inappropriate time (something I continue to do, much to my wife's chagrin). When I do those things, I now have a way to clean them up if anyone is hurt. I now have a relationship with a Power that has changed how I react to life. It is all good. Practice your practice. Find what works for you and your life, stay close to your Power, and help others along the way. With this outlook on life, you cannot fail.

As I go through my day, I stop when I am irritated or fearful and take a breath. I say my word or a short prayer that I know there is an energy of creation running this world that is not me. I ask to be put in a place where I can be of the most service and go with the flow. To practice genuine humility and take whatever comes along as part of the plan (not that I think there is a plan). I ask to live according to principle and shine my light wherever I go, never play small or big, to be what only I can be: myself. As Jen Sincero wrote in *You Are a Badass,* I ask to love myself with a kung fu grip. I want those things for you too.

Chapter Eight
No-Suck Rules for Living

"Contentment is the real wealth."
– Albert Noble

"I haven't failed. I have just found 10000 things that don't work." – Thomas Edison

What now? you may be wondering. *What comes after I have done the work and made the amends I can make? After I go out into the world and help others do the same thing, creating a world that revolves around service? After I have a meditation and inventory practice that helps me stay clean of any self-created conflicts or hiccups? After I have a spiritual life and I am living it daily? What now??*

That's not really my answer to give. I believe

you've got to see where the road is going to lead you. Mine led me here, to writing this book. I do not know where yours will take you, but I will share some of my adopted philosophies and practices. I did not create them, but I use them almost every day. I call them my rules for living a contented, useful life. You definitely don't have to treat them that way, though. As with anything else in this book, they are not intended to tell you what to do or how you should live (because I certainly do not know that)—they are merely things I have picked up along the way on my path that I want to share with you. Do what you will with them.

Stop making up stories. **Nothing is what you think it is**.

I make up stories all the time. I create scenarios and situations in my mind and attach meaning to them. Then I make decisions based on those stories and set about my life based on them. Here is a current example. I have a friend named Gerald. I called him a couple of times, but he did not return my call, so I sent him a text. Still, no response, it has been a couple of days, and I start to think something is wrong with our relationship; maybe he is mad at me or does not want to be my friend anymore, or he got in an accident and is in the hospital. I am really starting to get paranoid (another word for fear). *What could be wrong?*

I spent a couple of days in my head about it and finally got the message: I should try to call him back. He answers right away and is like, "Hey, dude, sorry I didn't call you back. I have been super slammed at work and wanted to take some time to chat." My story was never true, never had any relevance or truth attached to it, but I spent a couple of days wrapped up in my mind about it. None of the stories I make up in my mind are true ever, not once. But I have walked around in my life asleep, thinking I am awake, making things up all day long. I also make up stories about what other people are thinking, usually about me, which will be discussed later. But I knew it had to stop. All these stories were making me miserable; I was constantly in my head about them.

The thing that helps me to escape them is being in the now. Being in the here and now is the only cure for this. When I start to give in to the temptation to create a story about something, once I realize it, I check in with myself, say my phrase, and then look at the clock. I look at the date and I ask myself, "Tony, right now at this very moment, do you know that's the truth? Right now, are you okay? Is everyone in your family okay? Do you have everything you need?" Inevitably, the answer is I do not know if something is the truth unless I ask someone. Usually, I just fill in the blanks myself.

I am a stepparent; I have all kinds of stories about how my wife should parent her son. I make up all kinds of parameters in my head that demand that she behaves a certain way and parent her son how I see fit. I convinced myself that if she would only do it my way, then everything would be smooth as silk, and I spent an amazing amount of time trying to get it to be my way. I was demanding or sweet, depending on what and how I thought things should be. It got so bad that it really started to tear us apart as a couple. We decided that we needed some outside help with this issue and sought out some counseling. What became clear to me during that process is that I made up all these stories about how things needed to be. I made up all these rules in my head, and when my stepson did not adhere to them, I would create conflict with him and make my wife feel like she had to protect him. All of this because of a story I had created. So, I asked my Higher Power for a new story.

What came to me is that my *stepson has parents. I am not his parent. I am not in charge of what he does or does not do during the day or of anything, really. I am not responsible for his success or his failure. I am responsible for being a supportive and encouraging stepparent and friend if he wants one.* When I let go of the story that things needed to be my way or that he needed to act a certain way for me, our relationship dramatically improved. The conflict and tense energy in the house dropped exponentially. On top of that, my relationship with my wife has gotten so much better now that she doesn't feel like she has to constantly defend her son from me.

I lost a relationship this year because of a

story. It was heartbreaking, it still is painful, and I wish things had gone differently, but here is how it went. My buddy broke up with his fiancé for a reason I am not even sure about, but we were talking one day, and he told me he had broken up with her and she had moved out or was moving out. I thought that I should call her or text her just to make sure she was okay. I asked my wife first what she thought, and she suggested that I ask my buddy how he felt about me reaching out to her to check in with her. He told me that he felt that she would be fine, but did not tell me to not call her and I did not clarify how he really felt about it.

A couple of weeks went by, and I called him a few times in the span of a week, and he did not return my call. I sent him a text asking if everything was okay. He told me over text that he does not want to be in my life anymore because of my "obvious" feelings for his ex-girlfriend. I was extremely confused as I have never done anything inappropriate or out of line with her and am very committed to my wife and would never overstep anything that would make her feel uncomfortable. I texted him back and asked him if he wanted to have an actual conversation about this instead of texting. To which he replied that he was not interested in that and was moving on.

A couple more weeks went by, and I tried to call him again to discuss things, telling him how important our relationship is to me and asking how we could work it out. He never returned my call and is no longer in my life. He has made up his mind that the story he has about me is true. He never had a discussion with me about it; he just walked away. It still stings a little when I think about it. All of this could have been prevented, possibly with a conversation asking me for the truth. But we all gotta do what we got to do, and if anything does not belong in my life, it is cast out. The story ruined our relationship. Nothing else. None of it was true, nor is it true today.

Some examples could be when *so and so did this*, or *they did that because blah, blah, blah*. That is a story. We do not know why someone does or does not do something unless they tell us. Or we attach meaning to something: *I am angry at my wife for not supporting me emotionally. She does this to me because . . .* It is more accurate to say: *I feel like my wife does not support me emotionally, but in fact, she supports me a ton, just not always in the way I want. And if my happiness and contentment are based on how other people treat me or see me, I will never be satisfied. It will never be enough.*

The ever-present idea is that if we get enough of something or some magical gift from on high, it will satisfy us in some meaningful way or make us feel like we have finally gotten *there*. The truth for me is no destination has ever done so. No number of things or amount of money has ever fulfilled me as much as giving my most meaningful commodities to the world: my time, my energy, and my compassion.

I do not gossip until I do.

I believe the worst thing in the world is gossip. It is an awful and dangerous thing that can ruin people's lives based on no facts or research of what occurs in this world. It is my intent to never participate in gossip. I know that as humans, we all do it, but I have a mindset that means it is my intention to not repeat something, nor do I engage when someone says something to me. I never use my voice against someone else or against myself. I do not put myself down, nor do I put anyone else down, nor do I admonish someone else if they feel they need to gossip. I fail at this with my wife, often reprimanding her when I think she is breaking my rule. Sorry, honey. Here is my experience with a time when I gossiped about someone.

There was a person in my life whom I had developed a story about. He had never done anything to me personally, but I had developed a grudge against him because I was jealous. As I talked to one of his friends one day, I commented about him, saying, "I wouldn't want anything that guy has" in a very sanctimonious and condescending way. I went about my life, not even thinking about the comment I made about this guy. One day, he calls me and asks me for coffee. Of course, I say yes, and we meet up somewhere to catch up. By the way, this person was instrumental in an act that saved my life. This is and was an important figure to me. So, as we are having our cups of coffee, he asks, "I was wondering if I could ask you a question, Tony?"

To which I replied, "Of course." In a very calm and straightforward manner, he asked me if he had ever done anything to harm me, if he had ever said something hurtful to me that he was unaware of. He was curious. I replied, "No, I don't think so. Why?"

He says to me, "I'm just curious why you would say something like you said about me to this person? Why would you do that?"

My jaw must have dropped all the way to my knees. I was so embarrassed. I might have told the truth. I did not know why I said what I said. I did want what that guy had. He had a very successful business; he was a go-getter, had money, and drove a nice car. I think he had more than one car. I told this person I was wrong for saying anything about him and asked for his forgiveness. I had just been put face-to-face with what integrity and what living by principles really look like. I decided that day that I would not use my voice against a person like that again. That I would cultivate mindful speech, even though I did not know that is what it was at the time. This was all long before I had my experience in the hospital and began searching for spiritual life. But the train was set into motion. Here it is where it is today.

Is it true?

Do I know beyond a shadow of a doubt that what I am about to say is the truth? Have I done the research to determine that the thing I am about to say to someone is true? I have been guilty many times of merely repeating so-called facts that I heard from someone or got off the internet. I will ask myself if I am just showing off by sounding important or being a know-it-all. When I use this as one of the filters for how I interact in the world, it provides a foundation for living honesty. It is not always easy, and I know that the most honest thing I can say is that I am dishonest, but I practice being truthful.

Is it necessary?

As I may have mentioned earlier, I am the king of inappropriate comments at the most inappropriate times. I have a unique skill for dropping the f-bomb at the church picnic. I have, on many occasions, totally embarrassed my wife with some socially inappropriate thing that comes out of my mouth. This is one area in my life that has needed the most work. I have always felt that it was a sort of character asset and thought people could just shove off if they did not like it. Which, in fact, they certainly did. The most challenging thing has been for me to practice this in my daily life. But as I practiced it and fewer and fewer people ran out of the room when I was there, the more I saw its benefit. I attempt to ask myself as often as possible when speaking if what I am saying or about to say needs to be said, and if it needs to be said, does it need to be said by me. I do not always do it but find that it has never failed to help when I can apply it to my daily life. I have never been crucified for something I did not say. Often these days, I find the principle of restraint to be the most helpful for me. Which usually means I keep my mouth shut much more often.

Is it kind?

Once I have determined if what I am about to say is true and it's necessary to be said by me at this moment, I ask myself, is it kind? Am I thinking of how what I am about to say can affect others, or am I just trying to hear myself talk? Is what I am about to say going to add to the situation or make it worse. If I can answer yes to all these questions and I am not spreading gossip, it is okay to say what I will say. Trust me, I fail all the time at this. It is for me a guideline to operate out of or an ideal to live up to with the help of something bigger than myself, because self-help sucks.

What people think of me is none of my business.

I spent a good portion of my life worried about what other people were thinking about me. I would dress a certain way, do my hair a certain way, and change how I spoke, all to appease what I thought people were thinking. I once faked a Southern accent for a while because I believed people would think I was cooler and women would find me sexier. I would monitor everything through the filter of "what will they think?" and hardly ever thought about what was true for me or what I wanted to be or say or what kind of clothes I wanted to wear, for God's sake.

I know it's programming, and from an early age, we are taught to be consumed with what other people might be thinking about us, our image, and how we might look to them. Our whole social fabric is filled with this ideology. We want to look good, sound good, and feel important. No one wants to be a pariah. I am not suggesting that you not take a shower, not wash your hair, or not wear clean clothes. What I am suggesting and what I am attempting to live by is the principle of getting rid of the story and concluding that I might know what people are thinking or that what people are thinking is my business. Or that they are actually thinking of me at all. If I am acting outside of the bounds of integrity, honesty, and love, then I should probably be concerned with what other people are thinking. It could help me ask the Power to get me back on track and live according to my principles.

Once I am living the way that feels right to me, I cannot go around this life worrying or making decisions based on what other people may or may not be thinking. I must live by my heart and from my soul, principles, and actions. I want to look at myself in the mirror and feel good about myself, feel good about the person I am and the path I'm on. I can't do that if I constantly make decisions based on what I think others might be thinking. I cannot worry about that, even though sometimes I still do.

I am not interested in your opinion of an experience you have not had. Or mine.

Many people want to tell you what they think and share their political opinions and religious beliefs. They want to tell you how you should live or what you should do with your life. Yet if pressed about their experience, they have nothing to offer. They have only made up an opinion to make their ego or whatever feel comfort in believing they know what is best for this world or even best for themselves. I, myself, have spent a fair amount of time wasting my mental energy forming opinions on

135

the news, on world leaders, and on all kinds of topics I have never tried.

For most of my life, I have spent my time all throughout my day having opinions about things I have never done or may never do. I make judgments about everything, especially if I have not done them. I make judgments about politics, religion, people's hair, how they dress, how they raise their kids. I judge what I should or should not do, which keeps me from ever really attempting anything.

A year ago, I had a coaching session when my coach suggested I write a book bringing these principles forward to the world. I came up with all kinds of reasons (opinions) about why I could not do it and why I should not do it; I came up with many ways to do nothing. As the year went by, the more I did not do anything, the more I had opinions about all this stuff I had never done. Then the day came when I knew I had to write this book. I knew it was what I was supposed to do, but I had no idea where it was going, no idea if it would provide any kind of financial support for my family, but I did it.

Now I am having a new experience. Because

that is what I am interested in. I am interested in your experience. How did the book go that you wrote? What was your process? Did you publish it yourself or go through someone else? Oh, you never wrote or published a book? Okay, thanks for sharing, but I am not interested in your opinion. I do not have to be rude, but when someone offers me some advice or opinions about something, I can ask, "What did you do? What was your experience?" When they do not have any experience with something, it gives me permission to put it where it belongs. Sometimes, people will share their intuition, and that is a much different thing. It is usually filled with possibility and encouragement in statements like, "Why don't you just give it a try?"

I had all kinds of reasons earlier in my life why I could not give God a chance, why it would not work for me, and how guys like me are not spiritual people. Blah, blah, blah. But the truth is I never tried it. I never applied it to my life. I guess I thought I was too cool, or I thought I was too bad for God. There is a song lyric about how this grace thing works: it's what happens when all of your bridges get burned. Once I attempted the spiritual life, I began to have an experience with God. I began to see my demeanor change along with my reactions to life; I began to feel this thing inside of me that loves, all on its own, almost as if it is part of me, independent of me, with its own life force. So nowadays, when my magic brain tells me something, I ask myself, "What is your experience with this, Tony?" If I have none, I ask the mind to be quiet, say my word or phrase, and move on. I do not live that way anymore.

It is about the journey, not the destination.

I have been told that there are two ways to be unhappy: not getting what you want and getting exactly what you want. I have repeatedly set my sights on some goal or the acquisition of something that usually costs a ton of money and convinced myself that once I achieve that goal or get that thing, I will be satisfied and happy. Not to say that you should not have goals or set your intentions toward abundance and success because you should. But for me, the point is I have spent all this time trying to achieve some arbitrary goalpost, and once I get there, I have been disappointed with how I felt once.

Imagine you are a nomad traveling through the desert. Off in the distance is a shining gold city in the mountains that you have decided has everything you have ever needed. You are walking on the path, and surrounding it are people cooking, eating, and talking to one another. You have your sights so focused on your destination of the golden city that you do not stop along the way to meet any of these people or to eat. The journey is long and arduous, uphill, and wearing holes in your shoes. At some point, you discarded your pack because it was too heavy, but it had your bedding, blanket, snacks, and water in it. You keep walking with this shining golden city in your sights. It seems to be getting closer. You are convinced that it will provide everything you need and wealth beyond your wildest dreams once you get there.

As you get closer and closer, the people begin to disappear, the smells of food are fading away, and your water canteen has run out of water. Yet, you continue toward the city, on and on. Finally, you climb up the last hill, and you have arrived in the golden city of your dreams. You have worked so hard to achieve your goal. You have given up food and water and given up community and companionship to get to your goal. You arrive in the city, and it is so shiny and bright from the sun's rays shining off the golden walls, it looks incredible.

As you walk through the city streets, you notice that there is no one there; all the houses are empty, the roads are abandoned, and only trash and debris are blowing through the streets. Everything has been ransacked, anything of value has been taken off the walls. Every trinket or statue that could be of value or sold is gone. All that is left are the empty buildings and dirty streets. You wander around more and realize that you are hungry and thirsty, but there is no water anywhere, nor can you find any food, and you got rid of your backpack long ago. How you wished you had stopped along the way and talked to someone or eaten some of their food. You think how during your journey, you missed the beauty of the people and the desert and the last water in the oasis because you were so focused on your goal that you did not take any time to enjoy where you were or enjoy the people you met all in the name of getting there.

It is essential for me to take in the scenery along the journey, stop and eat and meet people along the way, drink when I am offered water, and notice what is right in front of me instead of solely focusing on getting there. Set your goals, set your intentions, make your vision board, write down your deepest desires and goals, including the financial benchmarks and things you want in your life. Envision all of it, write it down in your favorite notebook. Go out and try your hardest to make it all happen, please.

Meet your fellow people going the same and different directions as you, stop along the way, have a sandwich, drink a glass of wine or water, and enjoy where you are. Because once you get to where it is you have set your sights on or made that achievement, you may find, as I have, it wasn't as great as you thought it would be. Your magic mind will come up with yet one more thing to acquire or goal to achieve for it to be satisfied. No matter how much you get or how many achievements and accolades you get, there will always be another one. Always.

I have all these medals from the races I have done hanging in my bathroom over my toilet. That is how important they are to me. I have not gotten to a place where I can throw them away, but they don't mean much on their own. What they represent and remind me of consistently is that all of this is a journey. There is no destination, no final podium or award or achievement that will finally make me feel good enough. The journey to acquire those medals required day-in, day-out training, doing intervals when I did not feel like it, when it was cold and all I wanted to do was watch movies and eat a casserole. I did the work. Along the way, I got to see some progress. I got to see myself make excuses for not doing the workouts I missed.

As it was happening, I could not see myself transform physically, mentally, or spiritually. Still, when I pulled out photos of myself before I started the journey, I did not look good. I was overweight and did not feel and look healthy. I look at myself now, and I am happy with how I look; I am happy with how I feel. While I still race and enjoy racing, I only have about five or six races a year. The training is six days a week, four days on the bike, three days of core work, and one day of lifting weights—all of that for five races that I may not even do well in or get a flat tire or get dropped in to end up coming in last.

I am not doing it for glory, and I am not doing it to hang another medal in my bathroom, and all those days of training sure don't add up to those five races. Why do I do it? I do it because I am enjoying the journey. I take in the scenery along the way and coexist for a while with the people I meet on the path and we share our journeys. If I get to win or stand on the podium, that is a nice bonus, but it cannot be my focus. It will be highly disappointing if that is all I have to work toward.

And now, I have been on this journey a few times. As with bike racing, someone shows up who knows less than I do, and I get to show them some things that I have learned, share some mistakes and some failures, help them, and encourage them along the way. I also know they must do their own work. I cannot do it for them; they must do their own writing and inventory and make their own amends. I can get in the car and drive them, but they must knock on the door themselves. I cannot do it for them.

Stop being sorry.

I was reminded recently to not say I am sorry if I have done nothing wrong. I was talking to a woman about a topic that needed some elaboration and felt that I had taken up too much of her time. After I finished talking, I apologized for being so long-winded. She told me she had one rule to work with people, and that rule was that I could not be sorry if I had done nothing wrong.

She suggested that instead of apologizing, I should merely thank her for listening to my story and hearing me. I was floored and impressed. I realized how much I have been programmed in this world to be sorry, not feel like I am good enough, and apologize for everything from bumping into someone to using my voice or being myself. It really made me reflect on my life and how I want to be in this world. Not everyone is going to like me or approve of what I am doing, and honestly, if everyone likes you, you are being dishonest or a kiss ass.

So, I agreed to her rule for our relationship and vowed with God's help to make this a rule for myself moving forward in this life. I am not going to be sorry for things I have not done. *Stop saying it. I do not really mean it.* I can say excuse me or thank you or if I have harmed someone by my behavior and make amends. This is new for me and will more than likely need some practice. See how it feels for you and practice it in your life too. Let us be the change we want to see in the world.

Chapter Nine
The End Is Not the End?

Now this is not the end. It is not even the beginning of the end. But it is, perhaps, the end of the beginning. – Winston Churchill

What we call the beginning is often the end. And to make an end is to make a beginning. The end is where we start from. – T. S. Eliot

We read a book to my daughter that she loved so much as a three-year-old girl that she constantly asked us to read it to her. The title of that book is *Everybody Poops*. The premise is simple enough: animals, people, and every other living thing on this planet poops. No matter who we are or our station in life, we share this biological function. No one is above it, nor can they escape it; poop will happen no matter what. If you are one of the lucky ones, it will be consistent and not too dramatic (trust me, you do not want to experience flares).

We are all the same. We are made of the same material and have the same biological functions. At the same time, we are all different and have unique personalities, and each of us carries something out into the world that can help someone else. I may be the only example of what living a spiritual life looks like that someone ever gets to see. I know I am not above anyone, nor is anyone above me. We all sit on the toilet every day. No matter who we are, we all have our own values and insecurities that make us unique as a people.

The thing is that there is no getting *there*, no magical place that transcends the everyday trudging and living we all must do. We all must get up and put on pants and floss our teeth and go out and live our lives the best we can. So do your best and practice the principles that have been laid out here and see how your life transforms. Watch other people change their lives and help them whenever you can. Be yourself, love yourself, and give yourself a break. Walk down the path with your head held high, shining your brightness as you go to others along the way.

It is my heart's desire to contribute to this world, and if sharing these principles in this way helps someone, anyone, well then, I have done my job. I still think *self*-help sucks, but help from God and the Universe is real and tangible in my life. I hope that if something has your life in a mess and you can't seem to change it on your own, you will try this work and, in turn, show someone else how you did it. One person leads to the next, and the world becomes a more loving and beautiful place.

Remember, *self*-help sucks! But you don't.

Tony Blankenship is a former chef, spiritual seeker, and punk rocker. All the great insights in his book Self-Help Sucks, come from his own challenge of confronting and losing in his own struggle with addictive behavior. Using the principles and actions of the twelve-step program, Tony lays out his experience and some opinions that ultimately lead to the promise of inner peace and contentment. Tony lives in Santa Fe, NM. He is married with one daughter, a stepson, two dogs, two cats, two goldfish and a beta. When he is not writing he is an avid cyclist and amateur road bike racer. Tony passionately believes that if anyone does the work outlined in this book, they will address any of their destructive habits or addictive behavior. You can connect with him at tonyblankenship.com.

Made in United States
Orlando, FL
22 November 2021

10610173R10098